Peterson's egghead's Guide to Vocabulary

Cara Cantarella

About Peterson's Publishing

Peterson's Publishing provides the accurate, dependable, high-quality education content and guidance you need to succeed. No matter where you are on your academic or professional path, you can rely on Peterson's print and digital publications for the most up-to-date education exploration data, expert test-prep tools, and top-notch career success resources—everything you need to achieve your goals.

For more information, contact Peterson's, 800-338-3282 Ext. 54229; or find us online at www.petersonspublishing.com.

Bernadette Webster, Managing Editor; Ray Golaszewski, Publishing Operations Manager

ISBN-13: 978-0-7689-3661-2

ISBN-10: 0-7689-3661-6

Printed in the United States

10 9 8 7 6 5 4 3 2 1   15 14 13

Table of Contents

Chapter 1

Before You Begin

Welcome to *egghead's Guide to Vocabulary*! My name is egghead, and I'll be your guide thoughout the book.

This egghead's Guide was designed to help you learn vocabulary in a fun and easy way. Sometimes learning can be . . . well, boring. It can also be confusing at times. If it wasn't, we'd all have straight A's, right?

As your guide through the adventure of education, I'm here to make things a bit more enjoyable. I studied the boring books so you don't have to. I got straight A's and lived to tell about it. I understand this stuff, and you can too. In this guide, I'll show you what you need to learn to get to the next level.

Wherever I can, I explain things in pictures and stories. I break concepts down and teach them step by step. I try to stick with words that you know. I give examples from real life that you can relate to.

I want you to succeed, and I know you can do it!

In this book, we'll work together to improve your vocabulary and build your confidence. Confidence is very important, and it comes from trust. You can trust me as your guide, and most important, you can trust yourself. If your word knowledge isn't strong enough, let's do something about it!

How this book is organized

This book contains six chapters. We recommend you read them in order.

Chapter 1 is the introduction. You're reading that now!

Chapter 2 contains 100-level words. These are the first words you'll need to know.

Chapter 3 contains 200-level words. These are a little more difficult. They may appear in textbooks, literature, and on tests.

Chapter 4 contains 300-level words. These are the hardest words in the book. Learn these if you're preparing for a standardized test. They may come up on the SAT* and other tests.

Chapter 5 contains common prefixes, suffixes, and roots.

These word parts can help you with the meanings of words you don't know.

*SAT is a registered trademark of the College Board, which was not involved in the production of, and does not endorse, this product.

Chapter 6 contains practice exercises.

Complete the games to practice what you've learned. The more you use the words, the better they will "stick" in your mind.

Practice makes perfect!

To learn more

Ready to learn more words? After you've finished this book, visit the egghead website at www.petersonspublishing.com. Click the egghead link for even more new words and practice. This book will get you off to a great start. The website can give you that extra vocabulary boost!

Find us on Facebook

You can find us on Facebook® at www.facebook.com/petersonspublishing. Peterson's resources are available to help you do your best in school and on important tests in your future.

Peterson's books

Along with the egghead's Guides, Peterson's publishes many types of books. These can help you prepare for tests, choose a college, and plan your career. They can even help you obtain financial aid. Look for Peterson's books at your school guidance office, local library or bookstore or at www.petersonsbooks.com. Many Peterson's eBooks are also online!

Before You Begin

We welcome any comments or suggestions you may have about this book. Your feedback will help us make educational dreams possible for you—and others like you.

Now that you know what's ahead, let's get started!

Chapter 2

100-Level Words

You gotta know 'em!

Abstract: not concrete

Example

Physical objects are concrete. You can touch and hold them. Thoughts and ideas are *abstract*. You can't touch or hold them. Some *abstract* ideas are hard to understand.

Meet Robert

Robert was an artist. He liked to paint *abstract* art. Robert's friends liked him, but they didn't understand his art. Instead of painting objects like vases or flowers, Robert painted "ideas." They looked like blobs on a page.

It's art! Just let it flow over you!

Accessible: easy to access or understand

Example
Something that is *accessible* is easily entered or not difficult to figure out.

Hard to access

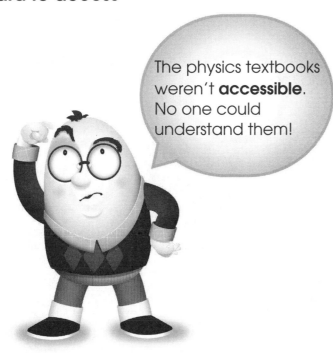

The physics textbooks weren't **accessible**. No one could understand them!

Adhere: to stick to or follow

Example
You can *adhere* a stamp to an envelope.
You can *adhere* to a rule.

To adhere or not?
Geraldo enlisted in the military. There were many rules to follow. Geraldo realized he wasn't much of a "rule" guy. He liked to do things his own way. "Why do I have to *adhere* to specific rules for everything?" Geraldo asked himself. "What happens if I don't?" Geraldo found out the next day when he was on latrine duty. He was forced to clean all the bathrooms!

Advocate: to stand up for; to support

Example
People *advocate* for causes they believe in. For instance, they might *advocate* for a charity that rescues lost pets.

Mr. Hudson takes a stand
Mr. Hudson was a lawyer with a strong record. He rarely lost a case. In court he would *advocate* for his clients and help them win.

ˈad-və-kāt

Ambiguous: unclear or vague

Example
Something that's *ambiguous* can have more than one meaning, you're not sure exactly what it means.

Clear as mud?
Sasha's teacher complained that she could not understand Sasha's essay. "This sentence is *ambiguous* to me. What is it supposed to mean?" she asked Sasha. Sasha read the sentence over. Even she didn't understand it. "Oh goodness," she said. "I see what you mean about it not being clear."

Ambivalent: not certain

am-ˈbiv-ə-lən(t)

Example

Someone who is *ambivalent* has two different feelings at the same time about something, yet they cannot decide which feeling is right.

Ari can't decide

Ari had a friend named Yvonne. He had *ambivalent* feelings about her. He liked her and disliked her at the same time. He wasn't sure which feeling was the strongest.

Animate: to bring alive

Example
A cartoon is an *animated* movie. The characters seem to actually be moving.

Coming alive
The scientists sat staring at the experiment. Both seemed to be in deep thought. Suddenly, one of them became *animated,* jumping up and running around the room. "I've got it—I've got the answer!" he said.

Animosity: hatred

Example
If you feel *animosity* toward someone, you strongly dislike them. A bitter argument can be full of *animosity*.

Strong dislike
The campers started to feel *animosity* toward the camp staff, which treated them unfairly.

a-nə-ˈmä-sə-tē

Apathetic: not interested

I don't care about the fact that I don't care about it!

Example
Someone who is *apathetic* has no interest in a project or activity. They don't care about it.

Couldn't care less
Alex was *apathetic* about the results of the school contest. "I couldn't care less," he told a friend.

Arbitrary: random; based on someone's choice but not specific rules

Example
Something that is *arbitrary* might seem like it was done "out of the blue." It might not make sense.

Better than random
The student made an *arbitrary* choice to hate the cafeteria food. She had not even tried it!

Articulate: to express or pronounce clearly

Example
When you *articulate* an idea, you express it in words.

Clearly stated
The audience listened as the speaker started to *articulate* his idea. Even though the idea had just come to him, the speaker was able to express it clearly.

är-ˈti-kyə-lət

Assert: to put forward; to declare to be true

Example
When someone *asserts* himself, he is putting his ideas forward in a strong way. An "*assertion*" is a statement or conclusion put forward as true.

Giselle asserts herself
"As an employee, I really need to *assert* myself more," Giselle told her coworker. "I have some good ideas about how to improve the business. I should make myself heard."

Authentic: real

Example
Something that is *authentic* is the real thing. It is not fake.

Are you for real?

The real deal
People want to feel that a writer is truly sharing his emotions when he or she writes. They want the writing to be an *authentic* expression of what the writer believes. This is part of what makes good writing so powerful.

Beneficial: good

Example
Something that is *beneficial* has positive effects. It is good for you.

A benefit for all
"My friend Alison is feeling down," Lisa thought. "I think I'll do something that is *beneficial* for both of us. I'll take us out to a movie."

Bolster: to support

Example
To *bolster* is to hold something up or support it. A wooden beam might be used to *bolster* a wall. It gives the wall support.

Strong support
The debate team had an excellent argument. They *bolstered* it with facts and clear examples.

Bureaucracy: a group that runs a government or organization

Example

City governments are often administered by large *bureaucracies* with many employees and departments.

Complex bureaucracy

The court system in Marin County is a complex *bureaucracy*. If you get a traffic ticket, you must go through a long process to have a hearing.

Calculate: to add; to find a value using math

Example

You can *calculate* the balance in your checkbook using a calculator.

It all adds up

The business owner *calculated* the day's sales. He was pleased about the total. Business was booming!

Be sure it all adds up!

Captivate: to hold someone's attention

Example

When you *captivate* someone, you capture their attention. They find you fascinating.

How interesting!

The boss explains

During the meeting, Evan was *captivated* as his boss spoke. He had always admired her and respected her business sense. He listened closely to what she said.

Catalyst: an influence that starts something else

Example

A *catalyst* is a person or object that puts something else in motion. A friend or teacher might give you an idea to take a class. That person would be the *catalyst* for your extended studies.

A great start

Billy's grandmother inspired him to become a doctor. She believed in him and helped him with each step. She was the *catalyst* for his career

Chaotic: very confusing, with little order

Example

Something that is *chaotic* is extremely disorganized. A sock drawer can be *chaotic* if everything is thrown in randomly. Sporting events can become *chaotic* if participants do not have set guidelines on how to play the game.

Chaos Rules!

So many speakers!

The meeting was highly disorganized. Everyone talked at once. The room was *chaotic*. It was very confusing.

Practice 1 – Matching Game

Directions

Here is an exercise to practice what you've learned. Match the words to their definitions below.

Definitions

___ **A.** not certain

___ **B.** to stick or follow

___ **C.** to find a value using math

___ **D.** very confusing, with little order

___ **E.** unclear or vague

___ **F.** good

___ **G.** to stand up for, support

___ **H.** to bring alive

Words

1. advocate
2. ambiguous
3. beneficial
4. animate
5. calculate
6. adhere
7. ambivalent
8. chaotic

You'll find the answers at the end of this chapter.

Coherent: clear and logical

Example
Something that is *coherent* is easy to understand. It makes sense.

I get it!

Albert stops to think
Albert was building a cabinet. He got the idea from a magazine article. Halfway through, he had to stop, because the instructions were so confusing. "This isn't going to work," Albert thought to himself. "I need a more *coherent* approach. The steps have to make sense. They all should be done in a logical order."

Cohesive: holds together

Example
Something that is *cohesive* sticks together. In a *cohesive* group, the members are unified.

A family affair
The Johnson family was a *cohesive* group. They stuck together and supported each other through thick and thin.

Collaborate: to work together

Example
When you *collaborate,* you work with someone else. Two people who write a song together *collaborate* on the song.

Working together
Ernesto agreed to *collaborate* with Gina on finishing their science fair projects. He was glad to have her help.

kə-ˈla-bə-ˌrāt

Colleague: a professional associate

Example
A *colleague* is someone you work with or know through your profession.

Nicole calls her colleague
Nicole had a *colleague* who owned several flower shops in the city. They had worked together at their first job. She called him to order flowers for her wedding.

Commerce: business

Example
E-*commerce* is business conducted over the Internet.

A business approach
"What do you think about my business idea?" Kari asked her friend Luke. She was about to start her own company. "It's an interesting approach to *commerce*," Luke said.

kəm-ˈpa-tə-bəl

Compatible: get along; go well together

Example
People who have the same interests may be *compatible*, because they like to do the same things.

We go well together
Darian was looking for a roommate. His friend suggested her brother, Ben. "You and Ben have a lot in common," Darian's friend said. "I think you'll be very *compatible* living together."

Compel: to force or strongly motivate

Example
To *compel* an action is to make it happen. When you are *compelled* to do something, you feel you must do it.

Three phone calls
Angeline was moving to Chicago. Three of her friends from high school lived there. Angeline felt *compelled* to call all of them the day she arrived to say hello.

Compliment: to say something nice to someone; a positive comment

Example
Zahara's boss really liked her presentation. He *complimented* her on it, telling her she did a good job.

Why, thank you!

Positive comments
Courtney's photography teacher commented on how much she liked Courtney's photographs. "Thanks for the *compliment*," Courtney said.

Comply: to give in or go along with

Example
To *comply* is to do what someone else wishes. When you *comply* with a request, you do what is asked.

Natalie agrees
Natalie wanted to paint her apartment. She asked her landlord if she could change the color of the walls. "OK, you can do it," the landlord said. Natalie was happy to learn that the owner had *complied* with her request.

Comprehensive: complete and total

Example
Something that is *comprehensive* covers everything. A *comprehensive* check of your car looks over the whole car.

A **comprehensive** check doesn't miss a thing!

Complete details
The catalogue was *comprehensive*, including every detail about the store's products. It listed all items the company sold.

Compromise: to come to a solution that all can agree on

Example
When you make a *compromise*, you agree on something that you are willing to accept, even if it doesn't have every aspect you truly want. Both sides usually give up something in a *compromise*.

James and Brenda agree
James and Brenda were meeting for dinner. James wanted to meet on his side of town, and Brenda wanted to meet near her house. Finally, they agreed to a *compromise*. They would meet in the middle.

Consequence: result

Example
A *consequence* is a result that follows from something else. If you drive too fast, you may get a ticket. The ticket is your *consequence* for speeding. *Consequences* can be positive, too.

Becoming rich is a **consequence** of saving wisely.

A great result
Harry was an extremely hard worker. He worked at his job for two years. One day, his boss called Harry into his office. As a *consequence* of Harry's hard work, his boss gave him a raise!

Conservative: moderate; not extreme

Example
Someone who is *conservative* acts with caution. They don't take a lot of risks. A *conservative* person might have traditional views. They stick with what is known and established.

More fence posts
The construction crew was building a fence at Walker's ranch. It seemed to take forever.

"How many more of these fence posts do we need to put in?" one worker asked.

"I'm not sure," the foreman replied. "As a *conservative* estimate," he continued, "I'd say about 150 more."

Constrain: to limit

Example

To *constrain* something means to hold it back. If someone breaks an arm and gets a cast, the cast *constrains* the arm. It keeps the arm from moving.

Removing limits

Richard was an interior decorator. He created a new design for his cousin Victor's living room.

"How much can I spend on the furniture?" Richard asked Victor.

"We don't want to *constrain* your creativity," Victor said. "Spend whatever it takes to do a great job!"

Contemporary: modern

Example

Something that is *contemporary* is current. It is happening now. *Contemporary* furniture is made in the present. It reflects current designs and styles.

Literature review

Anika was an English major. She studied American literature. She liked some historical novels, but she preferred *contemporary* ones. She could relate better to fiction from the present day.

kən-ˈtem-pə-ˌrer-ē

Context: the situation or environment in which something occurs

Example
Context is the "bigger picture" that a part or event fits into. For instance, a word is usually understood in the *context* of a larger sentence or paragraph. The sentence or paragraph provides the *context* you need to understand the word.

Bake sale surprise
Wanda and her mom organized a bake sale to raise money for the school hockey team. They set up outside the shopping mall. Sales were very poor.
"What does this mean?" Wanda asked her mother at the end of the day. "We spent all that effort, but we got no results!"
"You have to look at this in *context*, Wanda," her mom said. "Think about the big picture. We might not have raised much money, but we supported the team. It was for a good cause!"

Conventional: traditional, something that normally occurs

Example
Something that is *conventional* is common or expected. It is not out of the norm. A *conventional* approach, for instance, is an approach that people would usually take.

Not very ordinary
Alonzo loved to ski. Each winter, on his break from school, he would spend the entire vacation skiing.
"Alonzo, you're always going off to ski," his best friend Rick complained. "Why don't you join us and stay home for once?"
"Rick, you know I'm not a *conventional* guy. I have to do my own thing! I wouldn't be very happy staying home for the whole break like everyone else does," Alonzo said.

Convey: to tell or communicate

Take two aspirin and call me in the morning!

Example

To *convey* is to explain something or describe it. If you go on a trip out of town, you might *convey* instructions to a friend about how to feed your fish. A doctor might *convey* to you how to take care of a cold.

Gerald sends a message

Gerald worked in a busy office and rarely had time for breaks. If he wanted to communicate with a coworker, he usually sent a text message. It was often faster than *conveying* the message by phone.

Corrupt: to make something bad; something evil or unethical

Example

A *corrupt* government does not follow the laws. Leaders might take payments to avoid punishing people for crimes, for instance.

Good cop gone bad

The police officer discovered that her partner was *corrupt*. She overheard her partner doing business with a criminal.

Critique: to point out the flaws or bad points

Example
When an art teacher discusses a student's painting, he is *critiquing* that painting. *Critiques* often focus on bad points that need improvement.

krə-'tēk

Standing up to critiques
Carrie's sister had a hard day at the office. Her boss was not happy with her work. She did everything he asked, but he continued to complain.
"I know he's just stressed out now. I'm not going to take it personally," she told Carrie.
"I admire that about you," Carrie said. "It takes a strong person to handle other people's *critiques*."

Practice 2 – Fill in the Blank
Directions

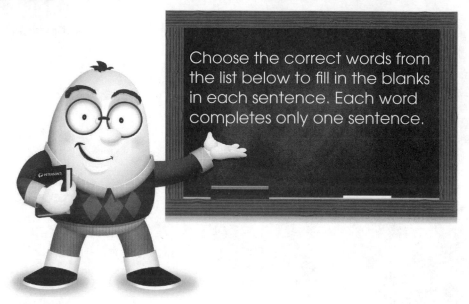

Choose the correct words from the list below to fill in the blanks in each sentence. Each word completes only one sentence.

Words

A. consequence

B. collaborate

C. context

D. compromise

E. conservative

F. compatible

G. convey

H. comply

Sentences

1. It is easier to understand what a word means when you read it in the _____ of a sentence.

2. Sarah did not like to take risks. She was very _____.

3. When you do what someone asks, you _____ with the request.

4. Two people who get along very well are _____ with each other.

5. If you run a red light, you are likely to get a ticket as a _____.

6. When two people conflict, they often solve problems by coming to a _____ that both can agree on.

7. When you _____ instructions to someone, you are telling them how to do a task.

8. When you work together with a friend, you _____ on the activity.

You'll find the answers at the end of this chapter.

Deceptive: lying, untruthful

Example

Someone who is being *deceptive* is telling a lie. A situation can also be *deceptive*. It is not what it appears to be.

Ain't it the truth!

A deceptive friend

Kyle found himself in an awkward situation. He believed his friend Turner was being *deceptive*. Turner said one thing, but his actions suggested that he was lying.

Deficient: lacking

Example

If you are *deficient* in vitamin C, you don't have enough of it. If your homework assignment is *deficient*, you might get a bad grade.

Pam's lesson

Pam received a grade of D on her history report. The teacher said Pam's report was *deficient*, because it lacked historical details.

Delete: to remove or take away

Example

When you are typing and you hit the backspace button, you *delete* a word. You erase it.

Wrapping up the project

"We should *delete* those computer files now that the project is over," the manager said. "We won't need them anymore."

Detach: to separate

Example

The word *detach* is the opposite of attach. When you attach two things, you bring them together. When you *detach* them, you pull them apart.

Eduardo pulls away

Eduardo was very excited about being in the school play. However, he did not get a part. He became very sad and *detached* after he learned the news. He didn't see any of his friends in theater for a while.

Differentiate: to tell the difference

Example

If you want to buy a new cell phone, you might research first to *differentiate* between the models. You would compare them to see what makes them unique. People also have trouble *differentiating* between twins. They can't tell them apart!

I'm egghead.

No, I'm egghead!

Real or not?

Some recordings sound so real, it's hard to *differentiate* them from an actual singer. It sounds like the singer is right there in the room.

Dilemma: a problem with two equally bad solutions

Example

A *dilemma* usually involves a problem with two solutions but both of them are undesirable.

Gilbert's dilemma

Gilbert had a *dilemma*. He saw his best friend Patrick throw a baseball and break their neighbor's window. But someone else blamed Gilbert. If he told the truth he'd lose Patrick as a friend. If he didn't, he'd get in trouble.

Discriminate: to tell the difference between two things; to treat someone differently because of certain characteristics

Example
People who *discriminate* against others leave them out or treat them badly. Some groups only admit members of certain races or religions. They *discriminate* against others.

A uniform policy
The school board did not want students to *discriminate* against other students because of their clothing. So, the board established a school uniform.

Dismay: sadness

Example
To be *dismayed* is to be disappointed. If you lose a contest, you might be *dismayed*.

Joel is dismayed
Joel practiced hard for the track meet. He was *dismayed* that he did not win first place.

Dismiss: to get rid of; to ask to leave

Example

When you *dismiss* a class, you let the students know they can leave. When you *dismiss* a thought, you stop thinking it.

Gabby's idea

Gabby was having trouble with her roommate. She thought about asking her roommate to move. Her roommate always paid the rent on time, though. Gabby *dismissed* the idea of looking for someone else.

Dispense: to give out

Example

A pharmacy *dispenses* medications.

You have to have a prescription, of course!

Giving good advice

Mr. Gooding was a counselor at Veronica's high school. He always *dispensed* good advice. Whenever Veronica had a question, she could count on Mr. Gooding to give a helpful reply.

Dispute: to argue; an argument

Example
When you *dispute* an idea, you argue against it. An insurance company can *dispute* a claim. That means they don't want to pay for it.

No argument here
Mr. Hawkins hit his neighbor's mailbox as he was backing out of his driveway. It could have turned into a big *dispute*, but it did not. Fortunately, Mr. Hawkins' neighbors were very nice about it.

Distinct: separate, unique

Example
Something that is *distinct* stands out from others. It may be unique, such as a *distinct* signature. Or it may just be separate from the rest.

That's very **distinct**!

A unique look
The giraffe has a *distinct* appearance. It is easy to identify because of its long neck.

Distinguish: to tell the difference between

Example
A jewelry expert can *distinguish* between a real diamond and a fake.

The twins
Greg and Ron were twins. Greg was two inches taller, so it was easy to *distinguish* him from his brother Ron.

Diverse: varied, different

Example
A zoo has a *diverse* collection of animals. There are animals of all kinds.

Quite **diverse**!

Varied interests
Crystal and her boyfriend John had *diverse* interests in movies. Crystal enjoyed science fiction and action films. John preferred comedies and historical dramas.

Domestic: having to do with the home

Example
Domestic chores are chores you do around the house. Cooking and cleaning are *domestic* chores.

Domestic or outdoors?
Ollie was *domestic*. He liked to stay in the house to read his war novels. Molly spent more time outdoors, because she played so many sports.

Dominate: to rule

Example
Someone who *dominates* rules or controls. A king *dominates* over his kingdom.

You rule!

The Cardinals win
Cody lived in St. Louis. He was a huge baseball fan. When the St. Louis Cardinals won the World Series 14-0, Cody was thrilled. "They *dominated* the game!" he said.

Elaborate: very involved or complex; to explain something in detail

Example
An *elaborate* wedding is one that has lots of expensive decorations.

Tara's lists
Tara kept *elaborate* lists of statistics about her favorite sports teams. The lists were detailed and complex. She liked to keep track of how the teams were performing.

Elated: very happy

Example
A student might be *elated* when she graduates from high school.

Her parents might be more **elated!**

A happy day
One day Janet came home from school and burst in the door with great news. One of her best friends was moving to her neighborhood. Janet was *elated*! She walked through the house with a huge smile on her face.

Enhance: to increase or improve

Example

You can *enhance* the look of a house by painting it.
You can *enhance* your chances of getting good grades by studying.

in-ˈhan(t)s

Marshall improves his chances

Marshall enjoyed running and decided he would run five days a week. He wanted to run in a five-mile race. Practicing regularly would *enhance* his chances of finishing the race.

Enterprise: a business or endeavor

Example

When you start a business *enterprise,* you begin a company or work endeavor.

A new business

Lydia owns a business selling women's clothes. It is a new *enterprise* that she just started last year.

Practice 3 – Synonyms

Directions

Match the words to their synonyms below.
Synonyms are words that mean the same thing.

Synonyms

___ **A.** thrilled
___ **B.** sadness
___ **C.** untruthful
___ **D.** improve
___ **E.** unique
___ **F.** control
___ **G.** remove
___ **H.** fancy

Words

1. deceptive
2. dismay
3. dominate
4. detach
5. elaborate
6. elated
7. distinct
8. enhance

You'll find the answers at the end of this chapter.

Error: mistake

Example
She made an *error* solving the math question. She got the answer wrong.

Fixing an error
Mr. Jackson was an excellent teacher. He did make mistakes sometimes as he was teaching. But whenever he made an *error,* he always corrected it quickly for the class.

Exclude: to leave out

Example
When you *exclude* something, you don't include it. You can *exclude* someone from a party, for instance. That means you don't invite them.

Exclude is the opposite of include.

Bryan is excluded
Bryan didn't like being *excluded* from teams at school. When people picked team members, if he wasn't chosen to play, he felt terrible.

Exempt: not required to do something

Example

If you are *exempt* from something, you don't have to do it. Some people are *exempt* from paying certain taxes.

How lucky!

Serena is exempt

Since Serena finished the semester early she was *exempt* from taking the final exam. She turned in a research paper instead.

Extravagant: unnecessarily large; too much

Example

An *extravagant* party might be one that costs too much or has more decorations than needed. An *extravagant* outfit is one that is too fancy or expensive.

A fancy party

Jasmine was at an *extravagant* birthday party for a friend. There were many people at the party, with lots of food and fancy decorations. There was even a pony! Jasmine was sure the party was quite expensive.

Fanatic: extremely devoted to something

Example
A *fanatic* is someone who is very devoted to an activity or cause. A movie *fanatic*, for instance, loves watching movies and watches them all the time.

The news fanatic
Reginald was a news *fanatic*. He watched the news nightly after dinner and read the paper each day. He talked all the time about current events.

Formulate: to create or put together

Example
A person might *formulate* a plan. They would think up the plan and put together its different parts. You could also *formulate* an idea or invention. Joseph Swan *formulated* the light bulb, but Thomas Edison made it work!

Laurel's plan
Laurel *formulated* a plan to save enough money for the car she wanted. She put a set amount away each month for a year. At the end of the year, she had enough to buy the car.

Foster: to support, nuture, or promote

Example
When you *foster* an idea, you help the idea develop.

Good relationships
Teachers often *foster* good relationships with students, so students can learn better.

Frank: direct, honest

Example

To be *frank* is to express yourself openly and directly. When a person is *frank*, he tells the truth in a clear way.

Mark speaks frankly

"Renee, can I be *frank* with you?" Mark asked his sister. Renee nodded yes. She wanted Mark to be direct and tell her honestly what he thought.

Frugal: not spending a lot of money; not costing a great deal of money

Example

A person can be *frugal* by not spending a lot on something, such as a meal. The meal itself might also be *frugal*, because it didn't cost much.

A frugal approach

Madison was *frugal*, like both of her parents. She never spent a lot on clothes or going out.

Habitat: living environment

Example

A *habitat* is a place where a person or animal lives. Wild animals might live in a jungle *habitat*. Certain birds are found only in the *habitat* of the rainforest.

I live in the **habitat** of the library!

Cheeky's habitat

Betsy had some food for her pet lizard, Cheeky. She put the food down in his aquarium which looked like a real forest, complete with mini trees. She and a friend had built Cheeky's *habitat* together as a science fair project.

Hypothesis: a theory, usually one that is tested

Example

When you make a *hypothesis,* you come up with an idea that you're not sure about. The *hypothesis* seems likely, but it hasn't been proven. Scientists create *hypotheses* and test them using experiments.

The doctor's hypothesis

The patient came in to the doctor's office with a strange illness. "I have a *hypothesis* about what this may be," the doctor said. "But I'd like to run some tests to be sure."

Identify: to determine or recognize

Example
You might *identify* which colleges you want to apply to by looking at a list and picking the ones you like best. You might also *identify* a person you know by recognizing a voice over the phone.

Jackie figures it out
Whenever Jackie's friend Steve tried to hide something he was feeling, Jackie always figured it out. She could *identify* whatever Steve was feeling. She knew him so well.

Identity: who someone is

Example
Mr. Thomson was approached by a person of unknown *identity*. Mr. Thomson had no idea who the person was.

Mistaken identity
Carly answered the phone and thought it was her friend Emma calling. After talking for a few minutes, Carly realized the caller was someone else. Carly apologized and said she thought she had been talking to Emma. It was a case of mistaken *identity*!

Imitate: copy

Example

When you *imitate* someone, you behave the same way that person does.

I'll copy that!

Chris imitates the teacher

Chris was asked by the teacher to solve a math problem on the board. He went through the steps of the solution for the class just as the teacher had done. He *imitated* her approach and got the correct answer.

Imply: to suggest

Example
Something that is *implied* is not directly stated. However, it is strongly suggested. You might *imply* that you want a certain gift by dropping hints.

Mrs. Montana implies
Kevin Hogan worked at Montana's, a family-owned feed store every weekend. Mrs. Montana had owned the store for 15 years. She was a tough boss. She liked to *imply* that Kevin should work harder. She never just came out and said it. But she dropped a lot of hints.

Incorporate: to include

Example
Something that is *incorporated* is included within something else. An exercise program might *incorporate* lifting weights.

Bringing it all together
Nancy was training to become a teacher. She decided to work as a student teacher while she went to school. That way, she could *incorporate* what she learned at school to help her students in the classroom.

Indecisive: not sure

Example
Someone who is *indecisive* can't make a decision. They might go back and forth between two options.

The customer can't decide
Ray was helping a customer buy a new lawnmower. He could tell the customer was *indecisive*. She couldn't seem to make up her mind. He gave her as much information as he could about the different mowers. Still, she couldn't choose which one to buy.

in-di-ˈsī-siv

Indifferent: not caring one way or the other

Example
Someone who is *indifferent* doesn't have an opinion about something. They don't support a specific viewpoint.

Sam is indifferent
Sam went to three job interviews. After all three interviews, Sam was clearly *indifferent* about the companies. He didn't feel strongly about any of them.

Integrate: to bring together

Example
Something that is *integrated* is unified. All of its parts are combined together as a whole. They are not separate.

Kendall's training
Kendall's boss was an expert woodworker. Kendall learned from her boss how to make cabinets. She *integrated* her new skills on every cabinet project.

Intuition: a gut sense about something

in-tü-ˈi-shən

Example
An *intuition* is a hunch or strong feeling. It's not based on facts or data. A mother using her *intuition* might look up just in time to see her toddler running out of the yard.

Jake has a hunch
At the county fair, Jake guessed the number of gumballs in a big jar. Jake guessed 500, and he won the game. The actual number was 501.

Jake's son Ryan was amazed. "How did you do that, Dad?" Ryan asked.

"*Intuition*, my boy," Jake said. "I just had a hunch. I thought it might be close to 500. And it was!"

Practice 4 – Antonyms

Directions

Match the words to their antonyms below. Antonyms are words that mean the opposite of each other.

Antonyms

___ **A.** include

___ **B.** indirect

___ **C.** certain

___ **D.** expensive

___ **E.** destroy

___ **F.** caring

___ **G.** correction

___ **H.** separate

Words

1. error

2. indecisive

3. frank

4. formulate

5. indifferent

6. exclude

7. frugal

8. integrate

You'll find the answers at the end of this chapter.

Irate: angry

Example
Someone who is *irate* is super angry.

Extreme anger
Rachel broke a vase while she was cleaning the living room. Her sister Tina frowned.

"Mom's going to be *irate* about that!" Tina said. "That vase is very valuable!"

Legitimate: legal, real, actual

Example
The king was the *legitimate* ruler of the country. His father had been king before him, and the throne was rightfully his.

li-ˈji-tə-mət

A very good reason
Brady was driving very fast. A police officer pulled him over.

"Sir, did you know you were speeding?" the officer asked.

"Yes, officer, but I have a *legitimate* reason," Brady explained. "My wife is having a baby!"

Liberal: generous, free; open-minded

ˈli-b(ə-)rəl

Example
He shared his opinions *liberally*, always telling people what he thought.

A little or a lot?
Maria was baking a cake. She read the cake recipe out loud before starting. Grease the pan *liberally* with butter or vegetable shortening, it read. "Grandma, what does *liberally* mean?" Maria asked.

"Well, back in my day, a *liberal* was someone who had very open-minded views," her grandmother responded.

"That doesn't make sense for a cake recipe," Maria said.

"*Liberally* also means generously," Grandma replied. "Use a lot of butter to grease the pan."

Mock: to make fun of

Example
You can *mock* someone by copying their behavior in a funny way.

Tabatha's wreck
Tabatha made a sculpture out of clay. She meant to make a horse, but it came out looking terrible. It looked like a bug with long legs.

Tabatha's brother *mocked* her when she brought the sculpture home. He tore a picture of a horse out of a magazine and put it next to Tabatha's sculpture. Then he burst out laughing. He liked to make fun of her any chance he got.

Moderate: in the middle; not extreme; relaxed

Example
He handled the argument in a *moderate* way. He did not get loud or upset.

A moderate result
Colin received a C on his English test. He was disappointed with the grade.
"I studied for that test," Colin said to his friend Arthur. "I should have done better."
"How hard did you study?" Arthur asked.
"Not terribly hard," Colin said. "But I did study some."
"Well, it makes sense then. You put in a *moderate* effort, and you got a *moderate* result," Arthur said.

Neglect: to not take care of something

Example
When you *neglect* something, you don't pay it attention or give it what it needs. A person can *neglect* a plant by not watering it enough.

Don't **neglect** to brush your teeth!

Sophia takes care
Sophia was a nurse in a busy hospital. No matter how many patients she had, Sophia was careful not to *neglect* anyone. She checked in on each patient regularly.

Objective: a goal; neutral; not taking sides

Example

Classes often have learning *objectives*. These express what you will learn by taking the course. In a court case, a judge is expected to make an *objective* decision based on facts, not emotions.

əb-ˈjek-tiv

No need to be fancy

Roger and Dina were building a shed for their tools. Roger paid a lot of attention to details, so the shed was taking a long time to build.

"There's no need to be fancy about it," Dina said. "The *objective* is to have a place to store our tools. It doesn't have to be the Taj Mahal!"

Opponent: someone you fight against

Example

When you play a game, the players on the other team are your *opponents*. You compete against them.

TV opponents

Mrs. Hartman really enjoyed cooking, even though she wasn't great at it. She liked to learn by watching the cooking shows on TV. Sometimes, there were contest shows where teams cooked together. The cooking team *opponents* would compete for the judges' votes.

Optimist: someone with a positive outlook

Example

Optimists expect good things. They focus on the positive.

On the bright side . . .

Ava was learning to knit. She made mistakes all the time when she first started. But she was an *optimist*. "Look on the bright side," she thought, "I've got a lot of time to get better."

Paradox: something that doesn't make sense; a statement that contains conflicting ideas

Example

Some common statements are *paradoxes*, "The silence was deafening," is one example.

Julian's paradox

Julian hurried to work on a cold, snowy Monday. On the way into the building, he ran into Dominic, who worked down the hall. Dominic was heading to Starbucks to get coffee.

"You're a fool to go out on a morning like this," Julian teased Dominic. "Your coffee will just get cold!"

"Well, if I'm a fool, I'm a wise fool," Dominic replied. He held up a huge thermos. He was going to pour his coffee in it to keep it warm.

"Good thinking," Julian replied. He thought about the concept of a wise fool. "That's really a *paradox*," he said to himself. "How can someone be foolish and wise?"

Perplex: to confuse

Example
Someone who is *perplexed* doesn't understand something.

I don't get it!

Ava is perplexed
Ava sat in trigonometry class watching her teacher write equations on the board. She was completely *perplexed*. It was so confusing, it seemed like her teacher was writing in Greek. In fact, some of the letters were Greek!

Persistent: continuing to do something; not giving up

Example
A person who is *persistent* stays focused on a goal and doesn't give up. Another example is a *persistent* cough. It just won't go away!

Estelle persists
Estelle was one of the youngest people at her company. She had become a partner in the business five years ago. The other owners made Estelle a partner because she was so *persistent*. She pursued every goal until she reached it. She never gave up, no matter what.

Pervasive: spread out everywhere

Example
Something that is *pervasive* is widespread or common. A *pervasive* belief is one shared by many. The flu can be *pervasive*, spreading quickly in winter.

A belief spreads
Someone made a false statement about Charlene. It simply wasn't true. Still, the story spread quickly around the school. Charlene and her friends wanted to stop the rumor from spreading, but it had become too *pervasive*.

Pessimist: someone with a negative outlook

Example
Pessimists expect bad things. They focus on what goes wrong.

Uh oh! Here comes trouble!

Expecting the worst
Audrey and Ali were going on a camping trip.
"My brother thinks it's going to rain," Audrey told Ali. "He thinks we'll have to come home early."
"Some people are such *pessimists!*" Ali said. "They always expect the worst!"

Plagiarize: to copy someone else's ideas or written words and present them as your own

Example
If you turned in a paper that someone else wrote, you would be *plagiarizing*.

ˈplā-jə-ˌrīz

A problem report
Mr. Sanders discovered that one of his students had *plagiarized* a research report. The student copied whole sections of an online article word for word and placed it in the report. This was shocking. Mr. Sanders didn't usually experience this type of behavior from his students.

Plausible: possibly true

Example
Something that is *plausible* makes logical sense. It seems to be true.

It could be true
Michele saw her friend Ingrid at the grocery store. Ingrid had just come back from England. Michele told her mother that she had run into Ingrid at the store. "But that's not *plausible*," Michele's mom said. "Ingrid's family is in England." "They just got back," Michele explained.

Plural: more than one

Example
The word "cats" is *plural*. It describes two or more cats.

Plural nouns and verbs
In a sentence, *plural* nouns are nouns that describe two or more things. If a sentence has a *plural* noun for its subject, it should also have a *plural* verb.

Popular: liked or wanted by many people

Example
A tablet app is *popular* if it has many downloads. The more downloads it has, the more *popular* it is!

That is a **popular** item. Everybody has one!

Policy changes
Penny was the head of the marketing department at her company. She made several changes that weren't *popular* with her staff. People didn't like the new policies at all. For some reason, the changes made them fear for their jobs.

Potential: the ability to accomplish or achieve a result

Example
Henry has the *potential* to succeed in business.

Potential for success
"This team has the *potential* to do very well this year," the manager told the sales team. "We have what it takes to reach our goals. If our sales numbers are strong, everyone will get a bonus. I want us to succeed!"

Precede: to come before

Example
In the alphabet, A *precedes* B.

After you!

Standing in line
Mrs. White stood in line at the check-out counter. She was *preceded* by three people with full shopping carts. She expected quite a wait.

Practice 5 – Fill in the Blank

Directions

Choose the correct words from the list below to fill in the blanks in each sentence below. Each word completes only one sentence.

Words

A. irate

B. mock

C. optimist

D. legitimate

E. perplex

F. plausible

G. liberal

H. precede

Sentences

1. If you are extremely angry, you are _____.

2. When you make someone confused, you _____ them.

3. The argument made logical sense and seemed likely to be true, so Tyrone thought it was _____.

4. Someone who is very open-minded is called a _____.

The answer to sentence No. 4 also means "generous."

5. Shana always looks on the bright side. She is an _____.

6. The company requires that all of its employees hold a _____ driver's license, in case they need to drive on the job.

7. To _____ someone is to make fun of her by copying her behavior.

8. The children are lined up in order from shortest to tallest. The shortest child will _____ the other children.

You'll find the answers at the end of this chapter.

Prevalent: widespread, very common

Example
Snow is very *prevalent* in winter.

They're everywhere
Apple trees are very *prevalent* in certain parts of the county. Almost everyone's property has one.

Procrastinate: to put something off until later

Example
If you *procrastinate,* you avoid doing a task.

Why put off until tomorrow what you can avoid doing entirely?

Megan gets to it
"I've got to finish my homework," Megan thought to herself. "I've *procrastinated* about it long enough. I don't want to put it off any longer."

Profound: very deep or moving

Example
You might have a *profound* experience listening to music that truly moves you.

A profound change
Kent was a house painter, and he recently quit his job. Leaving his job was a *profound* change for Kent. He decided to become a teacher.

Prosper: to do well, especially with money

Example
Someone who *prospers* does well in life. You can *prosper* by being successful or making a lot of money. You can *prosper* by being happy and fulfilled.

It's nice to **prosper!**

A prosperous time
The king told stories of hard times in his kingdom, before his family ruled. It was hard for some to believe that people in their towns had ever been poor. Ever since the king's family took the throne, the kingdom had been *prosperous*. There was plenty for everyone.

Provoke: to cause something to happen

Example
If you *provoke* a fight, you cause a conflict.

Provoking changes
At Warren High School, some students started skipping classes more often. This *provoked* changes in the school rules. The punishments became tougher for those who missed class.

Prudent: wise or reasonable; using good judgment

Example
A *prudent* decision is one that creates a good outcome. Someone who is *prudent* acts responsibly. The person is careful and thinks things through.

A wise choice
Zac was admitted to two colleges. One was far away from home, and the other was in Zac's home state. Zac chose the college that was close to his home. "That was a *prudent* choice," his mother said. Not only was the in-state school less expensive, it was a better college.

Qualify: to meet the requirements for something

Example
Beth was not *qualified* for the job. She did not have much experience.

I'm **qualified** to explain what **qualified** means. I've had a lot of experience explaining vocabulary!

Ethan is qualified
Ethan applied for a job as a computer programmer. The company was happy to hire him. He was highly *qualified* for the job and had the right amount of experience.

Rally: a group of people united for a cause

Example
The *rally* gathered outside the courthouse. Many people disliked the judge's decision.

A rally nearby
Perry looked out the window and saw a crowd gathering on the stairs of the capitol building across the street. He had forgotten that there was going to be a *rally* today. He put on his headphones to block out the noise.

Refute: to prove that something is false

Example
When you *refute* an argument, you show why it's not true.

Ellie agrees
Scott was used to arguing with his sister Ellie. She was captain of the debate team at school. She disagreed with just about everything Scott said.

"That was an excellent speech you gave," Scott said to Ellie after watching her team win a debate one afternoon.

Ellie's response surprised him. "I am not going to *refute* that," she said. "You're absolutely right!"

Relevant: important for a situation or idea

That's brilliant!

Example
When something is *relevant*, it applies to what you are focused on. A suggestion is *relevant* if it helps you solve a problem.

A relevant point
The professor was explaining a theory to students in his class. One of the students made a comment about the theory. It was a *relevant* point, so the professor stopped to discuss it.

Repulse: to cause to move away or draw back; to cause strong feelings of dislike

Example
A very ugly monster might *repulse* you.

Strong dislike
"That actor *repulses* me," Sylvia said as she was watching a movie on TV. "I just can't stand him."
"He's not that bad," Sylvia's friend Amber said. "Actually, I kind of like him."

Reserve: to set aside, to hold in advance

Example
You can *reserve* a table at a restaurant by calling ahead.

Money in reserve
The ABC Company held money in savings to keep the company running when business was slow. The savings fund was called the "*reserve* fund." The money was *reserved*, or set aside, as a backup.

Resolve: to solve or decide

Example
You can *resolve* a problem by finding a solution. You can *resolve* an argument by making up.

An argument resolved
Claire had an argument with her best friend Sally. They didn't speak for four days. At the end of the four days, they decided to talk. Fortunately, they *resolved* their differences.

Restrain: to hold back; to set limits on something

Example

When you *restrain* someone, you keep them from moving or acting.

I wanted two pieces of cake, but I **restrained** myself!

Matt holds back

Matt's father told him about a surprise he was getting for Matt's mom. Matt had to *restrain* himself not to give away the secret. He was so excited, he almost told her.

Retain: to keep

Example
To *retain* the cold air inside a fridge, don't leave the door open.

Retaining good staff
"One of our business goals is to *retain* the best employees in the city," the manager said at a meeting. "We want to keep the top people right here. To do that, we must create trust among the staff. If people trust us, they are more likely to stay with us."

ri-ˈta-lē-ˌāt

Retaliate: to fight back;
to hurt someone who has hurt you

Example
If someone plays a joke on you, you might *retaliate* by playing a joke on the person.

Avoiding retaliation
Christine asked Jeremy to keep the layoff meeting to himself. She was afraid that if employees knew that 100 people were going to be fired there might be problems. "If we tell others what happened in the meeting," Christine said, "they might *retaliate*. They might want to get us back in some way. We don't want to risk that." "I understand," Jeremy said.

Revere: to respect or admire deeply

Example
Someone who is *revered* is seen with great honor. A great queen might be *revered* by her people.

A great boss
At Will's job, there was one boss who everyone liked and admired. People *revered* him. They truly appreciated him because he had earned their trust.

Rigorous: difficult, challenging

No easy A's here!

Example
A *rigorous* school is one with hard classes. You can learn a lot, but you have to work for it.

A difficult year
The teachers at the school had gone through a *rigorous* year with many challenges. But they stuck with it and achieved their goals. All of the students at the school scored well on their state tests.

Routine: something done regularly, a series of actions always done the same way

Example
A dance *routine* is planned out beforehand. It is performed the same way each time.

Back to the routine
Over the weekend, Brendan enjoyed his free time. But when Monday arrived, he went back to his regular *routine* of school, football practice, and homework.

Sarcasm: saying the opposite of what you mean in order to hurt someone or make fun of them

Example
When you use *sarcasm*, you say one thing but you really mean the opposite. If a person always runs late, and she arrives late again, you might say, "I see you're on time as usual." What you really mean is "I see you're late as usual."

Less sarcasm
Cecelia heard a coworker talking about her. The coworker complained that Cecelia was difficult to work with. Cecelia decided to change her attitude. Over time, she used much less *sarcasm*. She stopped making negative comments about other employees.

Practice 6 – Reading Passage

Read the passage below and choose the correct answer for each question.

Passage

Astor Baker was headed to school one day when a friend stopped her on the road. "Hey, Astor," her friend said. "There's a rally in the school parking lot today after school. Want to join us?"

"What's the rally for?" Astor asked. She didn't want to miss cheerleading practice after school. Her squad was working hard to learn a new routine.

"We REALLY want the school to change the cafeteria menu. The food is so terrible. We hope a good crowd will catch their attention!"

Astor thought for a minute. Not only did she have cheerleading practice, but she had homework to finish, too. She had procrastinated doing her math assignment the night before and was planning to finish it before practice. Plus, she wasn't much of a "rally" kind of person. She preferred to resolve issues through discussion. A rally might provoke the school administrators to take disciplinary action. "I don't think so," Astor responded. "Don't you get worried that the administration might retaliate? They could slap us all with months of detention!"

"I know it might not seem prudent, Astor," her friend said. "There is always a risk they might try to get back at us. You know how nice they always are whenever anyone has a legitimate reason for being late."

Astor appreciated her friend's sarcasm. Maybe her math homework could wait until this evening.

Questions

1. **Which of the following statements is an example of sarcasm?**
   A. Don't you get concerned that the administration might retaliate?
   B. Maybe her math homework could wait until this evening.
   C. You know how nice they always are whenever anyone has a legitimate reason for being late.
   D. We REALLY want the school to change the cafeteria menu.

2. **Why was Astor planning to do her math homework before cheerleading practice?**
   A. She forgot that she had math homework until her friend reminded her.
   B. She had accidently left her completed assignment at home.
   C. She had put off finishing it the night before.
   D. She was planning to get help from a friend on the cheerleading squad.

3. **Which of the words from the passage most nearly means "wise or reasonable?"**
   A. Rally
   B. Prudent
   C. Routine
   D. Retaliate

4. **The word *provoke* in the passage most nearly means**
   A. To set aside
   B. To prove that something is false
   C. To meet the requirements for something
   D. To cause something to happen

5. How did Astor prefer to deal with conflict?
    A. Talking about it to work out a solution
    B. Using force to get a response
    C. Getting others to support her cause
    D. Avoiding conflict altogether

6. Which of the words from the passage most nearly means "to fight back?"
    A. Sarcasm
    B. Resolve
    C. Retaliate
    D. Procrastinate

7. Astor and her cheerleading team are most likely working on which of the following?
    A. Creating a new menu for the school cafeteria
    B. Hosting a very expensive party
    C. Organizing a group of teammates for an event
    D. Performing a series of moves always done the same way

8. The word *rally* in the passage refers to
    A. A meeting of several students with the principal
    B. A group of students who gather in the parking lot
    C. A friend who stops over at Astor's house
    D. A long walk to and from school

You'll find the answers at the end of this chapter.

Skeptical: doubtful

Example
Someone who is *skeptical* doesn't believe in something. They doubt it or question it.

Damien is doubtful
The president of the company promised everyone a raise by the end of the year. At first, Damien was *skeptical*. He doubted that the promise was real. But as time went on, he realized that the president's words were true.

Speculate: to predict an outcome

Example
If the sky looks dark and cloudy, you will probably *speculate* that it will rain.

Bring an umbrella!

The future outlook
The football team was having a bad season. Then it started to turn around. "How do you think the season will end up?" a sports reporter asked the coach at the end of a winning game.
"I don't want to *speculate* on how it will turn out," the coach said. "But it does look like we're doing better. The future seems a little brighter around here."

Spontaneous: not planned

Example

Something that is *spontaneous* occurs at the spur of the moment. It is not thought out. You might watch a movie *spontaneously*, for instance. You don't plan ahead—you just turn on the TV and there it is!

Esther gets spontaneous

One day, Esther asked her friend Marcus out to lunch unexpectedly. She came into his office and asked with no warning. Normally, Esther wasn't *spontaneous*. She usually made plans in advance.

Substantial: significant, a great deal

Example

Something that is *substantial* is "a lot." A *substantial* fortune is a lot of money. If a person has a *substantial* stake in a business, she owns a lot of it.

That's pretty big!

A substantial fortune

When Austin's grandmother died, he received some money she had left for him. It turns out, his grandmother was rich! She left Austin a *substantial* fortune. Now he was rich, too.

Subtle: not standing out;
not easy to see or sense

Example
A *subtle* sound is not easily heard. It is soft or faint; you have to pay attention to know it's there.

A subtle smile
The coach told Adam he had made the hockey team. A *subtle* smile crossed Adam's lips. The coach could barely see it, but it was there.

'sə-təl

Suppress: to hold back or hold down

Example
When you *suppress* your true feelings, you don't let them out. A government might *suppress* its people by being strict or controlling.

Marty keeps his cool
Marty's parents bought him a car for graduation. They gave him the keys at dinner. Marty *suppressed* the urge to jump up from the table and take the car out for a drive. He wanted to do that, but he held back.

Sustain: to keep something going, to support

Example

A singer who holds a musical note for a long time is *sustaining* that note. You can *sustain* a plant by watering it.

Keep up the good work!

Business holds steady

The hardware store owner was talking to a customer. "How's business?" the customer asked.

"We've been doing okay," the owner replied. "Business is pretty steady for us, fortunately. We have been open for 14 years, and we've always been able to *sustain* ourselves, even in tough times."

Tense: not relaxed

Example

Someone who is *tense* is very stressed out. A situation can be *tense* also. Something bad might happen.

A tense moment

Hassan asked his girlfriend Anna to marry him. He was a little *tense* because she did not respond right away. She looked at the ring without saying anything at first. Then she burst into a smile and said yes!

Tentative: not certain

Example
Something that is *tentative* might happen. It's not definite. You can make a *tentative* date with someone, for instance. You'll be there if all goes well, but you're not totally sure.

Joey responds
Joey was asked to be president of the chess club. He did not know whether he should accept. He was *tentative* when he spoke to the group. "Let me think about it," he said. "I have a lot going on with school right now. I think it will be okay, but I want to be sure before I commit to the job."

Terminate: to end

Example
When you *terminate* a contract, the contract ends. When you fire someone, you *terminate* their employment.

A new job role
Franklin was hired as a manager. "You realize, Franklin, that part of your job will be to *terminate* employees if necessary," his boss said. "You may have to fire people. Are you okay with that?"
"Yes, I can do it if I need to," Franklin said.

Toxic: poisonous

Example

Something that is *toxic* is harmful. Some chemicals are *toxic* when swallowed. They can cause damage or death.

A chemical that is **toxic** is called a toxin.

A non-toxic label

The label on the product states that it is not *toxic*. It is not poisonous to people or animals.

Trivial: small, not important

Example

A *trivial* detail is a minor detail. It's not necessary to know.

No trivial matter

Casey had been caught playing a trick on another student. He was sent to the principal's office.

"You know this is not a *trivial* matter," said the principal said to Casey. "It is very important."

"Yes, I understand," Casey said.

Uniform: the same, constant

Example
If two people have *uniform* views, it means they think alike. A business might have a *uniform* manufacturing process. It's always done the same way.

Always the same
The Lockland Company always did things a certain way. Its policies were very *uniform*. New employees had to learn the company procedures.

Valid: legal, true, logical

Example
A *valid* driver's license is legal and active. A *valid* point is reasonable. Logically, it makes sense.

That's correct!

Simon makes a purchase
Simon purchased some shoes from the mall. He paid for them with a check. "May I see some *valid* identification?" the store clerk asked.
Simon showed his driver's license, which was current. The clerk wrote down information from it and accepted Simon's check.

Versatile: capable of doing many different types of things; can be put to use for different purposes

Example

A piece of clothing can be *versatile*. It can be worn for casual or dressy events. People can be *versatile*, too. They may have multiple skills.

Bryce becomes versatile

When Bryce started at this company, he stocked items on the store shelves. He only knew how do to that one thing. Over time, however, he learned many aspects of the business and served in several positions. He became a *versatile* employee with many different skills.

Vulnerable: open to attack, easy to harm

Example

In the wild, deer are *vulnerable* to lions. Deer don't have sharp claws or fangs like lions do, so they can't protect themselves from attack.

Tonya is scared

On her way home from work, Tonya almost got in a car accident. She felt *vulnerable* because the roads were icy and it wasn't safe to drive. She drove very carefully the rest of the way.

Waiver: an agreement to give up the right to something

Example

When you sign a *waiver*, you give up your rights to that particular thing. If you participate in a dangerous sport such as skydiving, you might have to sign a *waiver* first. You agree that you won't sue the company if you get hurt. You give up your right to sue.

A waiver is signed

As companies begin to grow, they often hire more employees. They offer benefits, such as health insurance, to keep the best employees. Some new employees don't wish to take the health insurance. They sign a *waiver* stating that they give up the insurance.

Waver: to swing back and forth

Example

Someone who *wavers* on a decision changes their mind. First they take one position, then another.

I think so . . . but maybe not!

No wavering about this!

Luis was not sure what classes to take. He *wavered* between history and science. His friend Charles signed up for history, so Luis chose history, too. He finally made up his mind.

Practice 7 – Bucket Game

Directions

Group the words into the buckets below. Each word belongs in one of the buckets.

Word List
Skeptical
Subtle
Suppress
Tentative
Terminate
Trivial
Waver

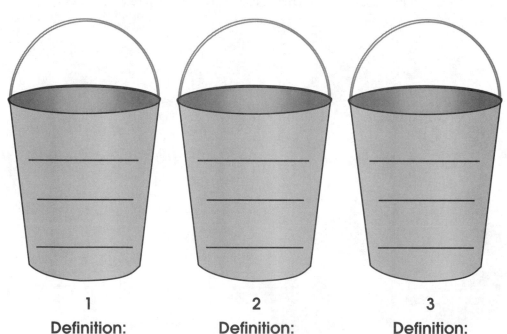

1

Definition:
Not sure about, undecided, or not certain

2

Definition:
Small, not standing out, or not important

3

Definition:
To stop, to hold back, or to end

Answers & Solutions

Practice 1 – Matching Game
Check your answers against the solutions below.

Answer Key
1. G
2. E
3. F
4. H
5. C
6. B
7. A
8. D

Explanations
1. **The correct answer is G.** *Advocate* means to stand up for or support.
2. **The correct answer is E.** *Ambiguous* means unclear or vague.
3. **The correct answer is F.** *Beneficial* means good.

Something that is **beneficial** is good for you.

4. The correct answer is H. *Animate* means to bring alive.

Cartoons are **animated** drawings.

5. The correct answer is C. *Calculate* means to find a value using math.

6. The correct answer is B. *Adhere* means to stick or follow.

7. The correct answer is A. *Ambivalent* means not certain.

8. The correct answer is D. *Chaotic* means very confusing, with little order.

Practice 2 – Fill in the Blank
Check your answers against the solutions below.

Answer Key

1. C
2. E
3. H
4. F
5. A
6. D
7. G
8. B

Explanations

1. **The correct answer is C.** *Context* is the situation or environment in which something occurs. It is easier to understand what a word means when you read it in the context of a sentence.
2. **The correct answer is E.** *Conservative* means acting without risk. Someone who is *conservative* acts with caution.
3. **The correct answer is H.** When you do what someone asks, you *comply* with the request.

Comply means to give in or go along with.

4. **The correct answer is F.** *Compatible* means to get along, to go well together. Two people who get along very well are *compatible* with each other.

5. The correct answer is A. A *consequence* is a result or an outcome. If you run a red light, you are likely to get a ticket as a consequence.

6. The correct answer is D. When two people conflict, they often solve problems by coming to a *compromise* that both can agree on.

To **compromise** is to come to a solution that everyone accepts.

7. The correct answer is G. *Convey* means to tell or communicate. When you *convey* instructions to someone, you are telling them how to do a task.

8. The correct answer is B. *Collaborate* means to work together.

Practice 3 – Synonyms
Check your answers against the solutions below.

Answer Key

1. C
2. B
3. F
4. G
5. H
6. A
7. E
8. D

Explanations

1. **The correct answer is C.** *Deceptive* means lying. Untruthful is a synonym of *deceptive*.

Someone who is **deceptive** is being dishonest.

2. **The correct answer is B.** *Dismay* means sadness. Sadness is a synonym of *dismay*.
3. **The correct answer is F.** *Dominate* means to rule or control. Control is a synonym of *dominate*.
4. **The correct answer is G.** *Detach* means to separate or pull apart. Remove is a synonym of *detach*. You can *detach* a post-it note from a mirror.

5. **The correct answer is H.** *Elaborate* means involved or complex. Fancy is a synonym of *elaborate*.

6. **The correct answer is A.** *Elated* means very happy. Thrilled is a synonym of *elated*.

7. **The correct answer is E.** *Distinct* means separate or unique. Unique is a synonym of *distinct*.

8. **The correct answer is D.** *Enhance* means to increase or improve. Improve is a synonym of *enhance*.

Congrats!
You've **enhanced** your vocabulary!

Practice 4 – Antonyms
Check your answers against the solutions below.

Answer Key

1. G
2. C
3. B
4. E
5. F
6. A
7. D
8. H

Explanations

1. **The correct answer is G.** *Error* means mistake. Correction is an antonym of *error*.
2. **The correct answer is C.** *Indecisive* means not sure. Certain is an antonym of *indecisive*.
3. **The correct answer is B.** *Frank* means direct. Indirect is an antonym of *frank*.
4. **The correct answer is E.** *Formulate* means to create or put together. Destroy is an antonym of *formulate*.
5. **The correct answer is F.** *Caring* is an antonym of indifferent.
6. **The correct answer is A.** *Exclude* means to leave out. Include is an antonym of *exclude*.
7. **The correct answer is D.** *Frugal* means not costing a lot of money. Expensive is an antonym of *frugal*.
8. **The correct answer is H.** *Integrate* means to bring together. Separate is an antonym of *integrate*.

Practice 5 – Fill in the Blank
Check your answers against the solutions below.

Answer Key

1. A
2. E
3. F
4. G
5. C
6. D
7. B
8. H

Explanations

1. The correct answer is A. *Irate* means angry. If you are extremely angry, you are *irate*.

Huh?

2. The correct answer is E. *Perplex* means to confuse. When you make someone confused, you *perplex* them.

3. The correct answer is F. *Plausible* means logical and possibly true. The argument made logical sense and seemed likely to be true, so Tyrone thought it was *plausible*.

4. The correct answer is G. *Liberal* means open-minded. Someone who is open-minded is called a *liberal*.

5. The correct answer is C. Shana always looks on the bright side. She is an *optimist*.

An **optimist** is someone with a positive outlook.

6. The correct answer is D. *Legitimate* means legal or real. The company requires that all of its employees hold a *legitimate* driver's license in case they need to drive on the job.

7. The correct answer is B. *Mock* means to make fun of. To *mock* someone is to make fun of her by copying her behavior.

8. The correct answer is H. The children are lined up in order from shortest to tallest. The shortest child will *precede* the other children.

Precede means to come before.

Practice 6 – Reading Passage

Check your answers against the solutions below.

Answer Key

1. C
2. C
3. B
4. D
5. A
6. C
7. D
8. B

Explanations

1. The correct answer is C. *Sarcasm* occurs when you say the opposite of what you mean in order to make fun of someone. When Astor's friend says, "You know how nice they always are…" to describe the administration, she really means the opposite. Most likely they are harsh when students are tardy. This statement is an example of *sarcasm*.

2. The correct answer is C. According to the passage, Astor had *procrastinated* doing her math homework the night before. This means she had put off finishing it.

Procrastinate means to put something off until later.

3. The correct answer is B. *Prudent* means wise or reasonable.

4. The correct answer is D. *Provoke* means to cause something to happen.

5. The correct answer is A. *Resolve* means to solve or decide. According to the passage, Astor preferred to *resolve* issues through discussion.

6. **The correct answer is C.** *Retaliate* means to fight back or to hurt someone who has hurt you.

7. **The correct answer is D.** According to the passage, the cheerleaders are working hard to learn a new *routine*.

8. **The correct answer is B.** *Rally* means a group of people united for a cause. In the passage, the word rally refers to a group of students who plan to gather in the parking lot.

Practice 7 – Bucket Game
Check your answers against the solutions below.

Answer Key

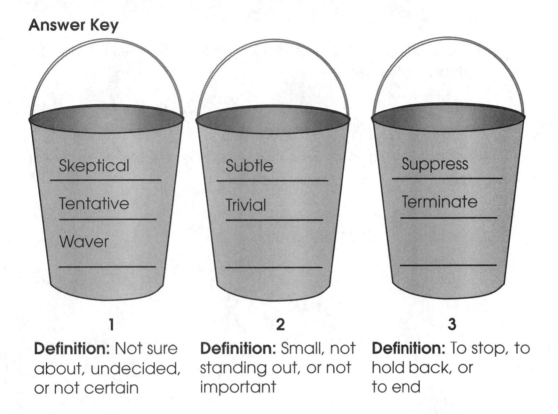

1	**2**	**3**
Skeptical	Subtle	Suppress
Tentative	Trivial	Terminate
Waver		

Definition: Not sure about, undecided, or not certain

Definition: Small, not standing out, or not important

Definition: To stop, to hold back, or to end

Explanations
Skeptical

Skeptical means doubtful. When someone is skeptical, they question something. They aren't sure about it. *Skeptical* belongs in Bucket 1.

Subtle

Subtle means not standing out. A light mark on a piece of furniture might be subtle. You might hardly notice it. *Subtle* belongs in Bucket 2.

Suppress

Suppress means to hold back or hold down. A cough *suppressant* stops you from coughing. *Suppress* belongs in Bucket 3.

Tentative

Tentative means not certain. Someone who is *tentative* is not sure about something. *Tentative* belongs in Bucket 1.

Terminate

Terminate means to end. The movie series called *The Terminator* is about a cyborg programmed to kill people. *Terminate* belongs in Bucket 3.

Trivial

Trivial means small or not important. The game *Trivial* Pursuit tests your knowledge of small details. *Trivial* belongs in Bucket 2.

Waver

Waver means to swing back and forth. If you *waver* on an issue, this means you change sides. First you might be for it, and then you might be against it. You're not sure about where you stand. *Waver* belongs in Bucket 1.

Chapter 3

200-Level Words

A little bit tougher!

Abstain: to choose not to do something

Example

When you *abstain* from something, you choose not to do it. You might *abstain* from eating sweets, for instance.

Couldn't we pick something else? How about **abstaining** from cod liver oil?

Jackie's choice

Jackie read that eating too much meat can be bad for one's health. To *abstain* from eating meat she became a vegetarian.

Acclaim: enthusiastic praise

Example

Acclaim is high praise. It is often given for outstanding achievement. An actor might get *acclaim* for making a great film.

Bravo!

The audience gave the opera singer much *acclaim*. They clapped and shouted "Bravo!"

Acumen: good judgment, know-how

ə-ˈkyü-mən

Example

The word *acumen* is often associated with business. A person with *acumen* makes good business decisions. They act quickly and accurately to deal with business matters.

Deal or no deal?

Steve used his business *acumen* to win the million-dollar account. After the meeting with the client, he acted quickly, rewriting his firm's proposal to meet the client's needs.

Adept: good at something

You are becoming **adept** with vocabulary!

Example

Someone who is *adept* is highly skilled. This person is well trained or knowledgeable. A master builder is *adept* at construction.

The Crossword King

Charlie's grandfather was *adept* at doing the Sunday crossword puzzle. He could solve it in fifteen minutes. His family called him the Crossword King.

Aesthetic: related to beauty or the way something looks

Example
The *aesthetic* of a room is the way the room looks. You might add some decorations to a room to improve its *aesthetic*.

A pretty picture
The painting was *aesthetically* pleasing. Carlos loved to look at it. It made the whole room look beautiful.

Alleviate: to lessen or make less

Example
When you *alleviate* something, you make it easier to deal with. Aspirin *alleviates* pain, for instance. It lessens the pain or makes it go away.

Help, Doctor!
Dorothy had a terrible back ache. She tried aspirin, but it didn't help. Finally, she went to the doctor. "Dorothy, I know just how to *alleviate* your pain," the doctor said. "You don't need any medicine."
"I don't, Doctor?" Dorothy asked.
"No! Just stop carrying your dog around in that basket!"

Allude: to hint at something

I'd like something green with presidents on the front.

Example
When you *allude* to something, you hint at it. You don't say it directly. You might *allude* to the fact that you would like a certain gift.

Just a hint
Michele told a story about one of her friends. She did not want to give the friend's name. Instead, she described the heroine as a brown-haired girl from Chicago, *alluding* to her best friend.

Altruistic: concerned with what is good for others

Example
People who are *altruistic* think about others. They are not selfish.

Doing for others
During Christmas break, a group of students went on a ski trip. Another group of students decided to stay home and do something more *altruistic*. They helped make a holiday dinner at a homeless shelter.

Anecdote: a brief story

Example
An *anecdote* is a shortened story. It may be funny or entertaining. You might tell an *anecdote* about something funny you experienced.

Sarah's stories
Sarah was always telling *anecdotes* about her mother in class. She had funny stories about their experiences together.

ˈa-nik-ˌdōt

Antagonize: to create conflict or bad feelings

Example
A cat might *antagonize* a dog. The cat might get just close enough to annoy the dog, and then run away.

The troublemaker
No one in the office liked the office manager. He was a real troublemaker. He *antagonized* the staff with his harsh comments.

Apprehend: to catch someone; to understand

I get your drift.

Example
To *apprehend* is to take someone into custody. The police might *apprehend* a thief for his crimes.
Apprehend can also mean to grasp the meaning of something. You might *apprehend* what a friend is saying to you.

Gotcha!
Florida police *apprehended* the bank robber after a routine traffic stop. Authorities had been searching for weeks and finally caught him thanks to a broken taillight.

Astute: Smart, clever

Example
A detective solves a mystery by being *astute*. He uses his smarts to figure out who committed the crime.

Really clever
The realtor was *astute* in getting a good price for our house. She was clever. We didn't think she could convince the buyers to pay so much, but she did!

Atrocious: terribly bad

Example
When your dog gets sprayed by a skunk, the smell is *atrocious*.

That's awful!
If someone sings off tune, it can sound *atrocious*. You try to be polite, but sometimes you can't help laughing. It's so terrible, it's funny!

Autonomous: independent

ò-ˈtä-nə-məs

Example
Infants cannot live *autonomously*. They depend on others to survive.

A free agent
When the police caught the suspect, they confirmed that he acted alone. He robbed the bank by himself and was completely *autonomous*.

Benefactor: someone who gives money or support for a cause

Example
A *benefactor* helps people in a way that benefits others. A wealthy person who gives money to a charity is a *benefactor* of that charity.

Bennie does good
Bennie was good-hearted person who gave a great deal of money to charities. He was the *benefactor* of many different causes. Each year, he chose a new charity to support.

Beneficent: kind, good

Example
A king who makes wise and caring decisions is a *beneficent* king. He rules in a way that benefits his people.

A kind leader
The leader of a country must maintain the country's respect. Some leaders gain respect by causing fear. Other leaders gain respect by making good decisions. It is better to be a *beneficent* leader than to rule by terror.

Benevolent: kind, good

Example
Someone who helps a stranger in an emergency may be a *benevolent* person. He is kind and good at heart.

Good-hearted
The owner of the corner store had a very good heart. She was caring and kind to her customers. They often spoke of how *benevolent* she was. She helped the neighborhood any way she could.

Benign: kind, good;
not harmful

Example
Some tumors in the body are *benign*. They do not spread or cause harm.

Pretty harmless
Spot was a dog with a loud bark. He seemed threatening, but actually he was very *benign*. He was all bark, no bite!

Bleak: plain or bare;
sad, not hopeful

Example
If the future does not look hopeful, we say the outlook is *bleak*.

A bleak day
When Old Mother Hubbard went to her cupboard, the cupboard was bare. That was a *bleak* day for the Hubbards.

Boisterous: noisy, with lots of activity

Example
The neighbors threw a *boisterous* party.

I didn't get any sleep last night!

Stop that noise!
A *boisterous* party might look like fun, but it can be tough on the neighbors. Some neighbors don't like it when a party gets noisy. They might call the police.

Practice 1 – Synonyms

Directions

Match the words to their synonyms below.
Synonyms are words that mean the same thing.

Synonyms

___ **A.** ease

___ **B.** bare

___ **C.** appearance

___ **D.** anger

___ **E.** good

___ **F.** understanding

___ **G.** loud

___ **H.** avoid

Words

1. aesthetic

2. boisterous

3. alleviate

4. abstain

5. bleak

6. antagonize

7. acumen

8. benign

You'll find the answers at the end of the chapter.

Candid: speaking the truth in a very direct way; telling it "straight up"

Example
A friend might speak with you *candidly*. They tell you exactly what they think.

Just sayin!

Speak candidly
The shop boss was difficult to work for. The workers were very unhappy. But during the boss' evaluation none of the employees were *candid* with the evaluators about his behavior. They were afraid they'd get fired!

Catharsis: to cleanse or make pure

Example
When she saw the sad movie, she had a *catharsis*. She cried for a long time and let her sadness go.

Complete cleanse
A good cry creates a *catharsis* or cleansing. Your emotions are released.

kə-ˈthär-səs

Cerebral: related to the brain

Example
Engineering is a *cerebral* subject.

It takes smarts to understand it!

Use your brain
Someone who is *cerebral* is interested in intellectual things. Scientists are often *cerebral*, as are mathematicians.

Charismatic: charming

Example
Dr. Martin Luther King Jr. was a *charismatic* speaker. His speeches touched people deeply.

Charismatic charm
Leaders who are *charismatic* make a good impression on people. President John F. Kennedy was a *charismatic* leader. His messages inspired the country.

Cite: to name a source of information

Example

You can *cite* an authority in a research report. This helps support your argument.

To cite or not?

Marley quoted an author in her research paper. She wasn't sure whether to *cite* the author or not. She asked her teacher to be sure. "If you use a quote, you should always *cite* the author," Marley's teacher said.

Clandestine: secret or hidden

Example

You might have a *clandestine* meeting. That means you meet in secret.

We can't keep meeting like this!

Hidden treasures

During the 1800s, slaves escaped from slavery through the Underground Railroad. The Underground Railroad was a *clandestine* operation. It was not an actual railroad, but a series of hidden routes that brought many slaves to freedom.

Coerce: to force

kō-ˈərs

Example
A bully might *coerce* others to give up their lunch money.

When push comes to shove
If force is used to obtain cooperation, this means the person is being *coerced*. The person doesn't want to cooperate, but is forced to.

Cogent: logical, convincing

Example
A *cogent* essay makes sense and is persuasive. You're likely to believe what it says.

A cogent plan
If you are a person who follows plans make sure your plans are *cogent*. They must make sense before you follow them. If they're logical, they might work!

Complement: to go well with something; to make something better or complete

Example
An outfit might *complement* someone. The outfit makes the person look great.

Very complementary
When two items go well together, they are *complementary*. Items such as peanut butter and jelly and bathing suits and flip flops *complement* each other.

Concede: to give in; to admit a loss

Example
In a contest, if you are losing, you might *concede* to the other person who has won.

Gary concedes
Gary ran for class president against Miranda. Miranda won by many votes. Gary was unhappy and asked that the votes be recounted. After the recount, Gary *conceded* to Miranda who had won.

I demand a recount before I **concede** the election.

Concise: short and to the point

Example
A sentence can be *concise*. It contains only necessary words.

Like this one!

Short and sweet
Some writers are known for being wordy. But in general, the best writing is *concise*. It conveys the most information in the fewest number of words.

Conform: to do the same as others

Example
You can *conform* to the wishes of a group. That means you do as the group does.

Conform to the norm
Many teenagers feel pressure to *conform*. The pressure may come from parents, religious groups, or friends at school. *Conforming*, if it goes against who you are, can be a problem at any age.

Contempt: hatred; looking down on someone

Example
When a person feels *contempt* for someone else, he looks down on them and dislikes them.

Great contempt
Adolf Hitler, the leader of Germany during World War II, had *contempt* for many races. He refused to accept those who were different.

Covert: hidden, not out in the open

ˈkō-(ˌ)vərt

Example
Spy operations are *covert*, as they are done in secret.

A covert call
During the mission, the spy used a small phone hidden in his pen. He talked quietly to keep the call *covert*.

Culpable: guilty or at fault

Example
A person who commits a crime is *culpable* for that crime. They have broken the law.

Guilty!
If you are guilty of a crime, and the court finds you are *culpable*, you may face jail time.

Cultivate: to help something grow

To **cultivate** good grades, it helps to study!

Example
You can *cultivate* a garden by taking care of it. One way to do that is by watering it to help it grow.

Thrive and grow
It is important to *cultivate* that which you care about. You might *cultivate* a relationship with someone, for instance. You spend time with them so the relationship can grow.

Practice 2 – Bucket Game

Directions

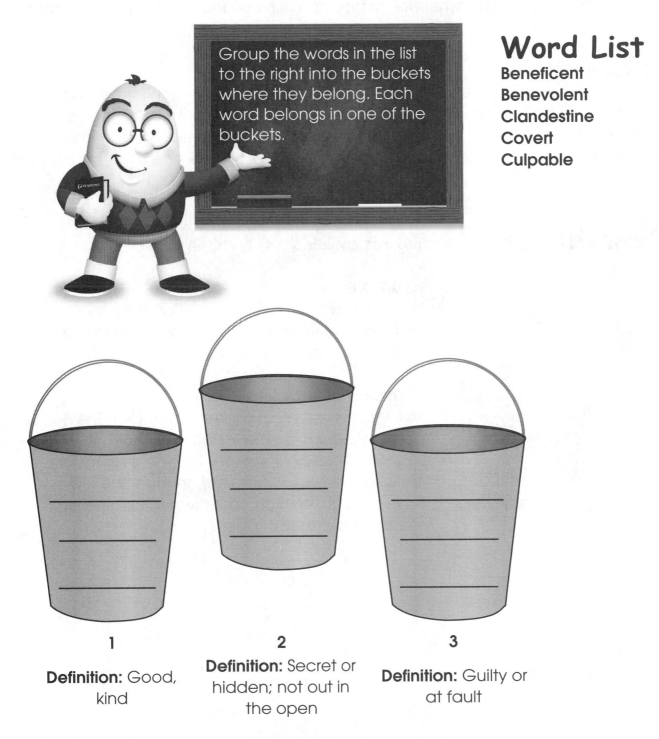

Group the words in the list to the right into the buckets where they belong. Each word belongs in one of the buckets.

Word List
Beneficent
Benevolent
Clandestine
Covert
Culpable

1

Definition: Good, kind

2

Definition: Secret or hidden; not out in the open

3

Definition: Guilty or at fault

You'll find the answers at the end of the chapter.

Cynical: believing that people are only out for themselves

Example

A person who is hurt by others might become *cynical*. They start to believe that all people are selfish.

Too cynical

Larry needed assistance with a building project. It was too much for him to do by himself. "You could ask one of the neighbors for help," Larry's wife suggested. "I'm not going to do that," Larry replied. "They're all just interested in themselves." "Larry, you're too *cynical*," his wife said. "Why don't you ask one of them and give them a chance?"

Dearth: a lack of something, not enough

Example

You can have a *dearth* of ideas about solving a problem. That means you have no clue how to resolve it. A *dearth* of funds means you lack money.

A dearth of supplies

Mrs. Major's class had a large art project. They were painting a mural on the school wall. Normally, Mrs. Major had plenty of supplies for whatever the art class needed. For this project, though, she did not have enough. With an entire wall to cover, there would be a *dearth* of paint!

Debilitate: to make weak

di-ˈbi-lə-ˌtāt

Example
An illness can *debilitate* you. It might make you weak and tired.

Overworked
Some students find it easy to read for hours on end. For other students, reading is *debilitating*. It really takes a lot out of them. After preparing for a big test, they want to do nothing but watch television and sleep!

Defer: to put off; to let someone else make a decision

Example
A business group might *defer* a decision until a later date. You might also *defer* to another person when choosing what to do about something. If that person has more experience than you, you might trust them to decide.

Let's defer it
The company executives held a meeting to plan for the next year. Donald, the CEO, brought up the issue of sales.

"Our sales are down since we stopped advertising," Donald said. "Is there anything we can do?"

Irene, the accountant, responded. "We are in the middle of running a budget report," she said. "We might have more funds for advertising since we've saved on other costs."

"Let's *defer* this discussion until we have the report next week," Donald said.

Definitive: the most complete and accurate; final

Example

The Guinness Book of World Records is the *definitive* guide to wacky achievements that people have done. It is the book with the most complete information about records people have set.

I hold the world record for the most books written by an egg.

Complete and accurate

It is hard to find a *definitive* source for history research. Every source seems to have its own opinions. If you are doing a research report, it's best to use several sources to check your facts.

Depict: to show or describe

Example

Photographs can *depict* people as younger than they really are. A story might *depict* a character as very unpleasant.

Depict the scene

A good author knows how to describe scenes in perfect detail. Scenes are *depicted* so well, you feel like you're in the room.

Dilate: to open wide

Example
When you are surprised, your eyes might *dilate*. This means they are open wide.

dī-ˌlāt

At the eye doctor
Jeremy went to have his eyes checked. At the end of the exam, the doctor said he was going to *dilate* Jeremy's eyes.

"What will happen?" Jeremy asked.

"I'll put some drops in that make your pupils widen," the doctor said. "It lets me see into the back of your eyes."

"Will it hurt?" Jeremy wondered. He was not sure about the idea.

"It won't hurt," the doctor said, "but you won't see as well for a few hours, because your eyes can't focus as easily. You shouldn't drive."

Jeremy called his dad, who took him out for ice cream after the exam. "I don't mind eye *dilation* so much after all," he thought.

Diligent: hard working; with great care

Example
A person who wants to earn more money might work *diligently* at his job. A *diligent* student is one who studies hard.

Working Extra Hard
Students of martial arts must work *diligently* to improve their skills. Mastery comes from consistent practice and focus so in order to obtain a black belt, students must truly apply themselves.

Discern: to see or identify;
to tell the difference between one thing and another

Example
A deer might *discern* a lion in the distance. That means the deer sees the lion.

To tell the difference
Rebecca had a sad face, so her friend Charlotte asked what was wrong.
"I thought I could trust Carla," Rebecca said. "But she just lied again."
Charlotte knew what Rebecca was talking about. Carla had lied to her, too.
"Becca, you've got to be more careful about who you pick as friends," Charlotte
said. "You have to *discern* who is really good for you. I wouldn't trust Carla one bit!"

Discord: conflict, disagreement

Example
Two countries might be in a state of *discord*. That means they fight a lot.

Fighting again?
Mrs. Smith and Mrs. Jones lived in the same apartment building. They were
constantly fighting. The other renters found their *discord* amusing. It was a little like
a skit from TV.

ˈdis-ˌkȯrd

Discretion: judgment, protecting privacy

Example

You can use your *discretion* to choose the best action in a situation. *Discretion* also means the ability to keep something private. If someone tells you something that is private and you don't tell anyone else, you are using *discretion*.

Using discretion

"Please don't tell anyone," Amanda said to Rudolfo. "I don't want anyone to know."

Amanda was moving to Hawaii, but she didn't want to break the news just yet. Rudolfo promised he would use his *discretion*. "Your secret is safe with me," he said.

Disparity: difference

There is a big **disparity** in size between an ant and a rhinoceros.

Example

There is a big *disparity* in sound between a flute and a tuba. In politics, groups often have *disparities* in their views.

Tell the difference

Rena and David were testing cakes for their wedding. They tried three samples, all chocolate.

"I can't tell the difference," David said.

"Are you kidding?" asked Rena. "There is a huge *disparity* between them! I noticed it right away!"

Dispel: to do away with

Example

When you *dispel* something, you make it go away. You can *dispel* a belief, for instance. That means you stop believing it.

Dispel that thought!

Some goals take time to achieve. It is easy to get discouraged if you don't see results quickly. However, it's important to *dispel* negative thoughts that might stop you. Just put the doubt right out of your mind!

Diverge: to go in different directions

Example

When you come to a fork in the road, the two paths *diverge*.

Divergent views

People who disagree often have *divergent* views. They see the issue differently. If their views are very far apart, they might just "agree to disagree."

Dogmatic: full of strong ideas

Example

When people talk about politics, they can become highly *dogmatic*.

The top dog

Lucas is the boss of a furniture company. He has very strong ideas about how furniture should be built.

Lucas had gotten angry with the production group. He gave them a *dogmatic* speech about quality.

"I don't get it," said one of his employees. "What's the big deal?"

"Lucas built this company by making great products," another employee said.

"We need to keep those standards. That's what our customers expect."

Duplicitous: lying, not telling the truth

du-ˈpli-sə-təs

Example

Card players who try to cheat are being *duplicitous*. They hide the fact that they are cheating.

A lying fool

Chip played cards with his friends every Sunday. One Sunday, a new player joined the group. He beat everyone all night. Chip saw the new player pull a card from his sleeve. Chip stopped the game and asked the cheater to leave. "*Duplicitous* players aren't welcomed here," Chip said.

Elite: of the highest quality or level

Example

Elite can be used to describe people. A top athlete who wins many events is an *elite* athlete. It can also be used to describe things. A car that is extremely well made might be an *elite* model, the top in its class.

Elite athletes

Professional athletes spend hours practicing their sport. Some *elite* weightlifters, for instance, practice three times a day, six days a week. That's a lot of heavy lifting!

Eloquent: good at speaking

Example

An *eloquent* speaker is someone who speaks powerfully. A graduation speech might be made by an *eloquent* speaker.

Dr. Martin Luther King Jr. was a charismatic and **eloquent** speaker.

Very eloquent

Good speakers can be very motivating. Dr. Martin Luther King Jr. inspired many with his *eloquent* speeches such as the "I Have a Dream" speech. It had a strong impact on civil rights.

Embellish: to add more detail

When I was a child, we had to walk five miles to school uphill both ways.

Example

When you *embellish* a story, you add more details to it. Sometimes when people *embellish* a story, they add details that aren't true. A grandfather might *embellish* a story he tells to his grandchildren.

Embellish that!

Some decorators like to *embellish* homes with enormous detail. I prefer simple decorations myself. It makes it easier to find what I need.

Empathy: understanding how someone else feels; feeling the same feelings as another person does

Example

Nurses often feel *empathy* for their patients. They understand how the patients feel.

I feel the same

Lamar and his grandfather went fishing. Lamar caught two fish, and his grandfather caught none. Grandpa was disappointed about his poor catch. Lamar had *empathy* for what his grandfather was feeling. He felt the same when he didn't catch anything!

Practice 3 – Fill in the Blank

Directions

Choose the correct words from the list to fill in the blanks in each sentence below. Each word completes only one sentence.

Words

A. dogmatic

B. discord

C. eloquent

D. embellish

E. discretion

F. elite

G. discern

H. dilate

Sentences

1. To constrict is to become smaller, and the opposite of constrict is _____.

2. The project was graded based on the teacher's _____.

3. It was difficult to _____ the difference between the two kinds of ice cream.

4. The company president was a/an _____ and inspiring speaker.

5. They were able to_____ the dress with many beads.

6. When the couple separated, there was _____ and conflict at home..

7. The leader was _____ whenever he argued about his principles.

8. When John got his bonus he bought a/an _____car; it was best in its class.

You'll find the answers at the end of the chapter.

Erratic: not regular; scattered or unpredictable

Example
A bird might fly in an *erratic* pattern.

Hard to predict
Norma's dog Harry loved going on walks. He waited for Norma to get home from work each day. Lately, Norma's work schedule had changed, making it unpredictable. Her schedule was so *erratic* that she sometimes walked Harry at midnight!

Exasperate: to really frustrate someone

Example
In a restaurant, a customer who complains all the time might *exasperate* the waitress.

Too frustrated!
If you have ever had a younger brother or sister, you know that they can be truly *exasperating*. They bug you about everything! Don't get too frustrated with them, though! Remember, you were once young yourself!

ig-ˈzas-pə-ˌrāt

Exemplify: to show something by example; to be an example of something

Example
Picasso was an artist who developed a style of painting called cubism. He painted many paintings in this style. Picasso's paintings *exemplify* the style of cubism.

For instance . . .
A customer ordered 30 pounds of chocolate from the Chocolate Store. It was the biggest order the store had ever had. When the customer came in to pick up the chocolate, she needed a cart to wheel it to her car.

"That's a lot of chocolate you have there," the sales clerk said as he helped her to her car. He loaded all the boxes in with a smile.

"Yes, I have a huge family," she said. "I always give chocolate for gifts. I shop at your store because you *exemplify* great customer service. Here—take a box of chocolates for yourself!"

Expedient: effective for producing a certain outcome

Example
If you are running late for work, it might be most *expedient* to skip your usual stop for coffee.

Works great!
Stephanie was efficient and liked to work *expediently*. If one method was more effective than another, she used the best method to reach her goal. She never took the long route when a shorter route would do.

Explicit: out in the open, not hidden; stated very directly

Example

You can give someone *explicit* instructions. The instructions are clear and direct. They state exactly what to do.

DO NOT FEED THE ZOO ANIMALS.

Out in the open

The basketball coach told each member to practice foul shots daily. She was *explicit* in explaining the technique. The team had no questions about how to shoot correctly.

Extraneous: not necessary;
not related to an issue or item

Example

Something *extraneous* is something extra that isn't necessary or important. An *extraneous* comment is not related to the subject being discussed.

It's not important

If you are the type of person who makes to-do lists, you might organize your list by what's most important. The first tasks on the list are those that have to be done. *Extraneous* tasks go at the end of the list. They're not really important.

Fallacy: false belief

Example

People used to believe the *fallacy* that the sun revolved around the Earth.

Just not true

A logical *fallacy* is a statement that does not follow from another. The statement is not valid, based on the reasons given. From a logical point of view, it's not true.

ˈfa-lə-sē

Fervent: passionate

Example

A person who supports a cause may be very *fervent* about it. They work at it with great passion.

Full of passion

Joyce was a *fervent* writer. She liked to write letters to the newspaper to express her opinions. Whenever something happened in town that Joyce did not like, she always wrote a passionate letter giving her views.

Futile: useless, pointless; doesn't do any good

Unless you have a gigantic shovel!

Example

If your efforts are *futile*, this means they don't do any good. It is *futile* to try to dig your way to China.

It's no use!

We had a broken lamp, and we tried and tried to fix it. But it was completely *futile*; the lamp could not be repaired. We gave up and bought a new one.

Gullible: easily misled; believes anything that's said, even if it's not true

Example
Young children are often *gullible*. They might believe what they are told, even if it isn't true.

That really happened?
Grandpa Barnes sat in his rocking chair and told a story of his time in the circus. He had been an animal trainer. "One time," Grandpa said, "a lion got out of his cage and bit me. I had to have 50 stitches."

Grandpa had a smile on his face, so I did not believe him. A bite with 50 stitches would have left a scar, and he didn't have any. "Grandpa, I'm not that *gullible!*" I said.

Illusion: something that appears real but isn't

Example
Magicians create *illusions*. They perform acts that appear to be real, such as sawing a person in half in a box. These tricks can't possibly be real, but they sure seem to be.

Optical illusion
Our eyes can play tricks on us. In the dark, a shadow can look like a monster. However, it's only an *illusion*.

Impede: to stop or get in the way of

Example
If you don't water a plant, you might *impede* its growth.

To slow or stop
Lorenzo was blind from birth. He loved music and wanted to play the piano. At first, he just banged on it and made awful noise. Soon his parents got Lorenzo a teacher, and they discovered he had real talent. His parents knew his blindness wouldn't *impede* his gift. Today he plays piano beautifully.

Impulsive: acting without thinking about it first

Example

People who are *impulsive* take action before they think. They act when an idea comes into their mind. Sometimes they do things they wish they hadn't done after all.

Great idea!

If you are an *impulsive* person, it's a good idea to have a big bank account. That way, when you see something you want, you'll have the money right there for it. You won't have to plan for it—you can just buy.

Indulge: to give in to one's wishes

Example

You might *indulge* yourself by having an extra scoop of ice cream. A parent could *indulge* a child by buying her a bike even if she already has one.

You get your wish

If you are impulsive and buy things without thinking, you might enjoy *indulging* yourself. But the purchases can pile up quickly. Along with a big bank account, you'll need a bigger house!

Inept: not able to do something

Example
Someone who is *inept* is not skilled.

Not very skilled
A person who's bad with numbers would be an *inept* accountant. A person who can't cook would be an *inept* chef.

Inherent: built in or a natural part of

Example
Skydiving is an *inherently* dangerous sport.

Built in
Some theories are *inherently* flawed. Take the popular theory that women are from Venus and men are from Mars. That's not true of course. There are no televised sports games on Mars!

in-ˈhir-ənt

Inhibit: to reduce or lessen

Example
Failure might *inhibit* some people from following their dreams.

Tom gets inhibited
Tom wanted to be an investor. He read books about the stock market. Once he even went to a class to learn more. Tom made mistakes at first, but he didn't let that *inhibit* him from continuing.

Innate: naturally a part of

Example
A genius is a person with *innate* extraordinary skill. Mozart's father was a musician. When Mozart was age five he began composing music. Mozart, it seems, had *innate* musical talent.

What is your **innate** talent?

An innate skill
Some people are *innately* thoughtful. They seem to know just what to say. They don't have to practice or run things through their heads. It comes out right the first time.

Innovate: to come up with a new approach; to create something new

Example

Technology companies often *innovate* to create new products. They come up with products that haven't been tried before.

Brand new ideas

Steve Jobs was an important technology innovator. He helped create Apple and Macintosh computers. He used his skills to *innovate*, creating the iPhone, iPod, and iPad.

Invoke: to call forth

Example

You can *invoke* someone's help. That means you ask them for support.

To call forth

The professor gave a talk about how writing came about. She *invoked* examples from ancient Egypt to explain why we use the alphabet.

Jovial: funny, good natured

Example
Someone who is *jovial* is in a good mood. They are happy and have a good sense of humor.

Full of cheer
My cousin Sam is very *jovial*. He is always full of cheer. Each year at the holidays, he comes over for dinner. He has everyone at the table laughing and smiling.

Keen: smart or sharp; excited about

Example
Someone with a *keen* wit makes good jokes. A *keen* eye for detail means that you notice details carefully. If you're not *keen* on something, it means you don't like it.

A keen wit
Comedians have *keen* wit. They know how to make funny remarks. Even if they haven't rehearsed it, they come up with something funny.

Lavish: full of luxury; done very "big!"; to do something in a large way

Example

You can throw a *lavish* party or own a *lavish* home. You can also *lavish* attention on a loved one.

What an outfit!

The movie star wore a *lavish* outfit complete with ruby tassels, diamond beads, and gold bangles to the opening of her new film. It was perfect for taking pictures on the red carpet. All the other guests wore *lavish* outfits, too!

Lethargic: slow and lazy; not active

Example

Someone who is *lethargic* doesn't have the energy to do much.

Slow and lazy

Even when cats are healthy, they often seem *lethargic*. They like to lie in the sun and sleep most of the day.

Practice 4 – Matching Game

Directions

Here is an exercise to practice what you've learned. Match the words to their definitions below.

Definitions

___ **A.** out in the open
___ **B.** built in or a natural part of
___ **C.** a false belief
___ **D.** full of luxury
___ **E.** passionate
___ **F.** to reduce or lessen
___ **G.** easily misled
___ **H.** smart or sharp

Words

1. inherent
2. keen
3. explicit
4. fallacy
5. gullible
6. lavish
7. inhibit
8. fervent

You'll find answers at the end of the chapter.

Lucid: clear;
having clarity

Example
A *lucid* dream is a dream that is clear. A *lucid* argument is one that makes sense.

Lucid thinking
Cheri was the manager of a busy store. But even when the store was super busy, Cheri gave good directions to the employees. Her instructions were always *lucid* and clear.

Malevolent: not good;
evil or bad-natured

Example
Someone who is *malevolent* has bad intentions. He wants to cause harm.

Many fairy tales have **malevolent** characters!

The evil wolf
In the story of Little Red Riding Hood, the wolf is a *malevolent* character. He dresses up like a kindly grandmother, but he has bad intentions.

Malignant: harmful;
quickly spreading and causing damage

Example
A tumor can be *malignant*. This means it is cancerous and is likely to spread.

Extremely Injurious
A virus on your computer can be highly *malignant*. It can damage all your files quickly.

Marginal: on the sidelines;
not central
so-so;
without much value

Example
The food at a restaurant might be *marginal*.

A marginal job
The bride hired a restaurant to provide food for her wedding. The restaurant did a *marginal* job. The food was just average, and the service wasn't great either.

Mediocre: average or "so-so"

I'll say! It's **mediocre.**

Example
If the food at a restaurant is marginal, you might also say it is *mediocre*.

It's so-so
The bride didn't want to ask her wedding guests how the food was. She knew it was *mediocre*. Even the groom thought it was just so-so.

Metaphor: using images or descriptions to show similarity between two different things

Example
Metaphors are often used in literature. Writers use *metaphors* when they describe something as if it were something else. "The child was a gentle little lamb" is one example.

Using metaphor
Writers use *metaphors* to make descriptions richer. A person might be described as "a real angel." This *metaphor* lets us know that the person is helpful and kind.

Mundane: ordinary; nothing special

Example
Something that is *mundane* has to do with everyday life. It's not exciting or special.

Mundane details
The article promised to give new information on the factors that caused the crime. But in reality, it only gave *mundane* details of the criminal's life. It talked about his past but did not explain what caused his actions.

Naïve: not very experienced; easy to fool

nä-'ēv

Example
A young person might be *naïve*. He hasn't had much life experience.

You can't fool me
Gabrielle went to her first dance audition Sunday. She felt a bit *naïve*. All of the other dancers seemed to know what to expect. They were much more experienced than Gabrielle.

Novel: new, unique

Example
The word *novel* means a book of fiction. It also means new or unique. For instance, you might have a *novel* idea. That means your idea is unique.

What a **novel** idea!

A novel technique
In order to create new ideas, designers must sometimes use *novel* techniques. Instead of drawing in a sketch book, they might draw in the sand on the beach. Or they might not do any drawing at all, instead speaking their ideas into a voice recorder.

Nuance: a difference that is small; it doesn't jump out at you.

Example
Sometimes, when you get your hair cut, the change is *nuanced*. You can hardly notice it.

Subtle and nuanced
"Do you notice something different about me?" Jane asked her boyfriend Conrad.

Conrad felt trapped. If he said no, Jane would get angry. If he noticed the wrong thing, she'd get angry too. He kept his mouth shut.

"Do you give up?" Jane asked. Conrad nodded. "Well, it's very subtle, but I did my hair a different way," Jane said.

Conrad breathed a sigh of relief. Now he could tell the difference. "It is pretty *nuanced*," he said, "but I love it. It looks great on you."

Obscure: not easily seen or understood; something out of the ordinary; to block the view of something

Example
You might have a shop that sells *obscure* items. The objects sold are hard to find and pretty unusual, like a saddle for a camel.

That's obscure!
Some books go out of print and are difficult to find. Fortunately, there are bookstores that specialize in hard-to-find titles. If you need an *obscure* book, you could try one of these.

Obsolete: outdated; no longer in use

Example
When something becomes *obsolete* it is no longer necessary to use. Ice boxes are *obsolete* now that we have refrigerators with freezers.

Out of date
Not long ago, music was sold on record albums. Today, albums are *obsolete*. Music is sold virtually and on CDs.

äb-sə-ˈlēt

Obstinate: stubborn

Example
Obstinate is a fancy word for pig-headed.

A stubborn pig?
Will was stubborn and would rarely change his mind. When he didn't want to do something, he could be *obstinate*. His wife often called him pig-headed. Will thought she was stubborn as an ox.

Opaque: not easy to see through

Example
A piece of glass might be *opaque* instead of clear. You can't see through it.

Opaque windows
The cathedral at the church had the most beautiful stained glass windows. They were *opaque*, so you couldn't see through them. But the rich colors allowed the light to shine through.

Overt: out in the open; not secret

Example
When people talk openly about a subject, they are being *overt* about it. They are sharing their opinions, not hiding them.

Completely open
"I have nothing to hide," the defendant said to the judge. "All of my actions have been completely *overt*."
"Then you maintain you did not break the law?" the judge asked.
"Yes I do, your honor. My business records show openly exactly what occurred."

ō-ˈvərt

Pedestrian: someone who is walking; something ordinary

Example
A *pedestrian* might cross the street in front of traffic.

Pedestrian crossing
At a busy intersection, there can be a great deal of traffic. Along with cars, you might see *pedestrians*, bicycles, and scooters. Occasionally you might even see a horse!

Peruse: to look over

I like to **peruse** *Vocabulary Today.*

Example

Peruse has two meanings. It can mean to look something over carefully. You might *peruse* a legal document before signing it, for instance. *Peruse* can also mean to look something over quickly. Basically, you just glance through it. In a waiting room, you might *peruse* a magazine.

Look carefully

Ellen hired a lawyer to help her establish her business. There were many documents to review. The lawyer *perused* them to be sure they were all accurate.

Philanthropy: helping people, especially by giving money to support a cause

Example

A *philanthropist* is someone who gives money to different causes.

The giving tree

Philanthropy usually involves giving money. But sometimes support can be given in different ways. *The Giving Tree* is a children's book about a tree that supports a boy in many ways such as giving him shade. The tree shares its own type of *philanthropy.*

Practice 5 – Antonyms

Directions

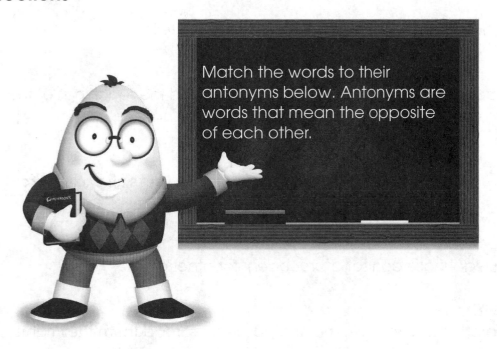

Match the words to their antonyms below. Antonyms are words that mean the opposite of each other.

Antonyms

___ **A.** kind

___ **B.** experienced

___ **C.** current

___ **D.** clear

___ **E.** agreeable

___ **F.** old

___ **G.** exciting

___ **H.** overlook

Words

1. mundane

2. obstinate

3. peruse

4. malevolent

5. novel

6. obsolete

7. opaque

8. naïve

You'll find the answers at the end of the chapter.

Pious: religious;
closely following religious ideas

Example
A person who is *pious* believes strongly in the principles of religion.

Very devoted
The priest was *pious* throughout his life. He always followed the teachings of the church. He set an example for others by his behavior.

Precedent: an event or decision that comes first and sets an example for what follows

Example
The decision in a legal case can set a *precedent* for other cases.

Legal precedents
When people are charged with a crime, the police must read them their rights. The civil rights are known as "Miranda rights." They get their name from a legal case called Miranda v. Arizona. In this case, the Supreme Court ruled that people must be informed of their rights if they are arrested. The case set the *precedent* for reading rights today.

Presume: to believe or suppose

Example
When you *presume* something, you believe it to be true—even though you don't know for sure.

I presume so
"Clarice, do you think it will rain today?" asked Redalgo. He noticed Clarice was carrying an umbrella.

"I *presume* so," Clarice answered.

"Why?" Redalgo wondered. "The sky is perfectly clear."

"The weather report said there was zero chance of rain," explained Clarice.

"Since the forecast is always wrong, I figure the chance is 100 percent!"

Proliferate: to grow in number; to expand or spread

Example
In the body, cells *proliferate* by dividing into new cells.

It spread!
Janelle noticed a new type of weed growing in her yard. She tried to pull it, but it just kept spreading. Finally the weed covered a large part of her yard. Janelle had never seen a weed *proliferate* like this one.

prə-ˈli-fə-ˌrāt

Propensity: tendency

Example
A person can have a *propensity* to behave in a certain way.

Santa Claus has a **propensity** to eat cookies and drink milk.

A propensity to succeed
James comes from a successful family. His family members succeed at all they do. Because of this, James believes he has the *propensity* to succeed, just like they do.

Proponent: supporter

Example
A *proponent* of an idea is a person who supports that idea.

Pro or con
A good plan cannot work without *proponents*. Even if the plan makes sense, it needs supporters to put it into action.

Query: question, inquiry

Example

When you ask a question, you are making a *query*. You might *query* a salesperson in a store.

Can you please tell me where to find the milk?

What's the question?

When you use a computer database, you obtain information through reports. The report provides a description of the data. In order to create a report, you must first give the database a *query*. The *query* is a question that asks the database for specific information.

Rebuttal: an argument that shows why another argument is wrong

Example

In a debate, the first team presents an argument. The second team argues against the first team's argument. The second team is presenting a *rebuttal*.

The right response

The debate team was good at creating arguments. But its greatest strength was making *rebuttals*. Whenever another team spoke, the debate team would present a strong *rebuttal*. The team made such a good argument against the other team that it always won.

Reconcile: to come back together; to make up

Example

When two people have a fight and make up, they *reconcile*.

Kiss and make up

Georgia and her boyfriend had a fight. It was the first one they'd ever had. Fortunately, it only lasted for two days. They *reconciled* quickly. They discovered it was more fun to make up!

Redundant: repetitive in a way that is unnecessary

Example

If you say the same thing twice in a row, you might be *redundant*.

I've heard that before

In his research paper, Jonah described how he conducted the science experiment. Later, in a different section, he described the experiment again. He used different words, but basically he said the same thing.
"Jonah, you can take this second description out," his teacher said when she read the paper. "It's really not necessary. You've already described the science experiment earlier, so it's *redundant* to explain it again."

Refine: to make better

Example
When you rewrite an essay to improve it, you are *refining* the essay.

New and improved!
Jonah took his teacher's advice and removed the redundant description. He polished up the paper and *refined* it. The final draft was much better.

Regimen: a strict program

Example
A diet is a type of *regimen*. A *regimen* could also be an exercise program, or a study plan.

A strict regimen
Leo was preparing for a boxing match. He needed to lose weight so he could qualify to compete. He went on a strict *regimen* of weight loss nutrients, mostly protein powders. It tasted terrible!

Repress: to press down or hold back

Example

The word *repress* is usually used when talking about feelings or ideas. You might *repress* your anger, for instance.

Don't hold back!

Skylar wasn't used to holding her feelings back. Her best friend Caroline was just the opposite. She *repressed* her feelings most of the time.

Resilient: bounces back easily

Example

A person who is always good natured is *resilient*. No matter what happens, she adjusts quickly and keeps a good attitude.

Resilient players

The theater group performed its first play of *Fiddler on the Roof*. The play got poor reviews. The players were discouraged, but their director cheered them up.
"I got bad reviews for my first four plays," the director said. "But then I won a Tony Award!"
The cast members were *resilient* and bounced back quickly. Their next play, *Grease*, got great reviews.

Rhetoric: speaking and writing effectively; speech or writing that is lacking real meaning

Example
When someone uses *rhetoric*, they "don't put their money where their mouth is." Their speech sounds good, but it doesn't have real substance to back it up.

Speech and writing
When voting for a political candidate, don't believe everything you hear. Campaigns contain a lot of *rhetoric*. Research wisely to know what the candidate truly stands for.

Scrutinize: to look at carefully

Example
A boss might *scrutinize* a financial report. He would review it carefully to make sure it was correct.

Scrutinize first
When you write a check, *scrutinize* it carefully before signing it. Make sure the dollar amount matches what is written.

Solicit: to ask

Example

When someone comes by your house and tries to sell you a magazine, they are a *solicitor*. They are asking, or *soliciting*, you to buy their magazine.

Would you like to buy a subscription to *Vocabulary Today*?

Solicit a favor

Rachel's car broke down on the highway. She stood outside and waved her arms to *solicit* help from cars passing by. Several people were happy to help. One even called a tow truck for her.

Sporadic: not occurring regularly

Example

Something that is *sporadic* does not occur in a predictable way. Instead, it is random. You never know when it might happen.

Completely random

Squirrels like to find nuts and hide them for the winter. They store them so they have food when they need it. Sometimes they find food in squirrel feeders, but this tends to be *sporadic*. The squirrels can't predict when the feeders will be full.

Stigma: a bad mark or association

Example

A *stigma* is an association with something that other people think is bad. In some countries, there is a *stigma* associated with following particular religions.

A bad mark

In the 1950s, the United States had a strong conflict with the Soviet Union. The Soviet Union had a communist government. If a group in the U.S. was suspected of agreeing with communist views, it might be investigated. Even today, among many Americans, a *stigma* is associated with belonging to a communist party.

Subsidize: to support by giving money

Example

The government *subsidizes* farmers who grow certain crops. They give farmers money to help maintain their farms.

Support story

Gerald wanted to go out on a date, but he was broke.
He really liked Daphne though, so he went to his father for help.
"Hey, Dad, would you be willing to *subsidize* my date with Daphne?" he asked.
Gerald's dad laughed. "If you mean will I give you the money, my answer is no. But I'd be happy to make you a loan!"

ˌsəb-sə-ˌdīz

Tedious: extremely boring or dull, due to lasting too long

Example

Something that is *tedious* lasts a long time and becomes boring. It is usually slow or repetitive.

That's tiresome

I find bowling to be a *tedious* sport. It does not hold much excitement for me. But it is not nearly as *tedious* as golf!

Tenacious: doesn't let go or give up; keeps on going no matter what

Example

Successful mountain climbers are *tenacious*. They keep going until they reach the top.

The tenacious hunter

A lion hunts its prey skillfully. He is *tenacious* in pursuing the prey he has chosen, never giving up even after chasing the prey for long distances. He also knows just the right moment to pounce.

Understatement: a description with less information or impact than the situation has in reality

Example
If you really like something, but you say it's only "okay," your description would be an *understatement*.

That's an **understatement.**

Understatement of the year
Some people like to brag, but others are prone to *understatement*. Henry and eight mountaineers worked through the night to rescue a dog left on the mountain by its owner to die. After the dog was safe at the vet, a television crew asked Henry if climbing at night scared him. "Scared," he cried. "That's an *understatement*. I was terrified."

Volatile: explosive; easily explodes

Example
Gasoline is highly *volatile*. If you light it with a match, it bursts into flames. Some people have *volatile* tempers. This means they are quick to anger.

It might explode!
Many garages have unsafe chemicals in them. It's important to review the labels of different products to see how best to store them. If a chemical is particularly *volatile*, it shouldn't be kept near a heat source. It might suddenly explode!

Practice 6 – Fill in the Blank

Directions

Choose the correct words from the list below to fill in the blanks in each sentence. Each word completes only one sentence.

Words

A. query
B. proliferate
C. tenacious
D. rhetoric
E. presume
F. solicit
G. volatile
H. propensity

Sentences

1. Raccoons have a _____ to dig through garbage at campsites.

2. If you _____ that a surprise party is being thrown for you, you might be disappointed if it doesn't actually happen.

3. When election season starts, there is a great deal of political _____ on TV.

4. Heather wanted to _____ help from her friend on the project.

5. The teacher answered Scott's _____.

6. The dog was _____ at trying to dig a hole under the fence.

7. The scientist expected the bacteria in the laboratory would _____ overnight.

8. People should not smoke around oxygen tanks because the tanks are highly _____.

You'll find answers at the end of the chapter.

Answers & Solutions

Practice 1 – Synonyms
Check your answers against the solutions below.

Answer Key

1. C
2. G
3. A
4. H
5. B
6. D
7. F
8. E

Explanations

1. **The correct answer is C.** *Aesthetic* means related to beauty or the way something looks. Appearance is a synonym of *aesthetic*.
2. **The correct answer is G.** *Boisterous* means noisy, with lots of activity. Loud is a synonym of *boisterous*.
3. **The correct answer is A.** *Alleviate* means to lessen or make less. Ease is a synonym of *alleviate*.

Reduce is also a synonym of **alleviate**.

egghead's Guide to Vocabulary

4. The correct answer is H. *Abstain* means to choose not to do something. Avoid is a synonym of *abstain*.

5. The correct answer is B. *Bleak* means plain or bare. Bare is a synonym of *bleak*.

6. The correct answer is D. *Antagonize* means to create conflict or bad feelings. Anger is a synonym of *antagonize*.

7. The correct answer is F. *Acumen* means good judgment or know-how. Understanding is a synonym of *acumen*.

8. The correct answer is E. *Benign* means kind or good. Good is a synonym of *benign*.

Practice 2 – Bucket Game
Check your answers against the solutions below.

Answer Key

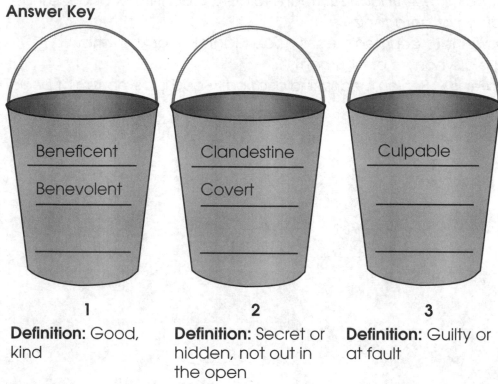

1

Definition: Good, kind

2

Definition: Secret or hidden, not out in the open

3

Definition: Guilty or at fault

Explanations

Beneficent

Beneficent means kind or good. *Beneficent* belongs in Bucket 1.

Benevolent

Benevolent also means kind or good. *Benevolent* belongs in Bucket 1.

Clandestine

Clandestine means secret or hidden. *Clandestine* belongs in Bucket 2.

Covert

Covert means hidden, not out in the open. *Covert* belongs in Bucket 2.

Culpable

Culpable means guilty or at fault. *Culpable* belongs in Bucket 3.

Practice 3 – Fill in the Blank
Check your answers against the solutions below.

Answer Key

1. H

2. E

3. G

4. C

5. D

6. B

7. A

8. F

Explanations

1. **The correct answer is H.** *Dilate* means to open wide. To constrict is to become smaller, and the opposite of constrict is *dilate*.

2. **The correct answer is E.** *Discretion* means judgment. The project was graded based on the teacher's *discretion*.

When you choose freely what to do, you are using your **discretion**.

3. **The correct answer is G.** *Discern* means to tell the difference between one object and another. It was difficult to *discern* the difference between the two kinds of ice cream.

4. **The correct answer is C.** *Eloquent* means speaking well. The company president was an *eloquent* and inspiring speaker.

5. **The correct answer is D.** To *embellish* means to add more detail. They were able to *embellish* the dress with many beads.

6. **The correct answer is B.** *Discord* means conflict or disagreement. The two neighboring countries were in constant *discord* with one another.

7. **The correct answer is A.** *Dogmatic* means full of very strong ideas. The leader was very *dogmatic* whenever he argued about his principles.

8. **The correct answer is F.** *Elite* means having the highest quality or importance. When John got his bonus, he bought an *elite* car; it was the best in its class.

Practice 4 – Matching Game
Check your answers against the solutions below.

Answer Key

1. B
2. H
3. A
4. C
5. G
6. D
7. F
8. E

Explanations

1. **The correct answer is B.** *Inherent* means built in or a natural part of.
2. **The correct answer is H.** *Keen* means smart or sharp.
3. **The correct answer is A.** *Explicit* means out in the open.

When someone gives you an **explicit** warning, they state the warning openly.

4. **The correct answer is C.** *Fallacy* means a false belief.
5. **The correct answer is G.** *Gullible* means easily misled.
6. **The correct answer is D.** *Lavish* means full of luxury.
7. **The correct answer is F.** *Inhibit* means to reduce or lessen.
8. **The correct answer is E.** *Fervent* means passionate.

Practice 5 – Antonyms
Check your answers against the solutions below.

Answer Key
1. G
2. E
3. H
4. A
5. F
6. C
7. D
8. B

Explanations

1. **The correct answer is G.** *Mundane* means ordinary or dull. Exciting is an antonym of *mundane*.
2. **The correct answer is E.** *Obstinate* means stubborn. Agreeable is an antonym of *obstinate*.

I agree that he's very **obstinate**.

3. **The correct answer is H.** *Peruse* means to look over. Overlook is an antonym of *peruse*.
4. **The correct answer is A.** *Malevolent* means evil or bad-natured. Kind is an antonym of *malevolent*.

5. The correct answer is F. *Novel* means new or unique. Old is an antonym of *novel*.

6. The correct answer is C. *Obsolete* means outdated. Current is an antonym of *obsolete*.

7. The correct answer is D. *Opaque* means not easy to see through. Clear is an antonym of *opaque*.

8. The correct answer is B. *Naïve* means easily fooled or not very experienced. Experienced is an antonym of *naïve*.

Practice 6 – Fill in the Blank
Check your answers against the solutions below.

Answer Key
1. H
2. E
3. D
4. F
5. A
6. C
7. B
8. G

Explanations

1. **The correct answer is H.** *Propensity* means tendency or likelihood. Raccoons have a *propensity* to dig through garbage at campsites.

2. **The correct answer is E.** *Presume* means to believe or to suppose. If you *presume* that a surprise party is being thrown for you, you might be disappointed if it doesn't actually happen.

3. **The correct answer is D.** *Rhetoric* means speech or writing. When election season starts, there is a great deal of political *rhetoric* on TV.

4. **The correct answer is F.** *Solicit* means to ask. Heather wanted to *solicit* help from her friend on the project.

5. **The correct answer is A.** *Query* means question or inquiry. The teacher answered Scott's *query.*

6. **The correct answer is C.** *Tenacious* means to keep at it, never giving up or letting go. The dog was *tenacious* at trying to dig a hole under the fence.

7. **The correct answer is B.** *Proliferate* means to grow in number and also to expand or spread. The scientist expected that the bacteria in the laboratory would *proliferate* over night.

8. **The correct answer is G.** *Volatile* means explosive. Something that is *volatile* easily explodes. People should not smoke around oxygen tanks because the tanks are highly *volatile.*

Chapter 4

300-Level Words

The toughest group!

Acquiesce: to give in

Example
To *acquiesce* is to agree to something, even though you might not really want to. Someone who *acquiesces* goes along without making a big deal out of it.

Micah gives in
Micah was not really interested in watching the hockey game. But his roommate Larry insisted. Micah decided to *acquiesce,* and he watched the game with Larry.

Adroit: skilled, nimble

Example
Professional athletes are very *adroit* at playing sports.

An adroit move
The football player caught the ball and ran toward the end zone. Just as he was about to get tackled, he made an *adroit* move and scored a touchdown.

Antithetical: opposed to

Example
Something that is *antithetical* is the exact opposite of something.

Two opposites
Abe and Gabe were brothers. You would never know it, however. Their personalities were *antithetical* to each other. Abe talked fast and was always busy with an activity. Gabe was relaxed and spent most of his time watching TV.

Apprise: to notify

Your toast is burning!

Example
You might *apprise* someone that the toaster is on fire.

Apprise me, please
If you rent an apartment, your landlord should *apprise* you when your lease is up. That way, you can decide if you want to leave or stay.

Assuage: to calm

Example
A bottle can *assuage* a crying baby.

Soothing the beast
In the fairy tale *Beauty and the Beast*, the Beast becomes very upset when Belle leaves the castle. He is only *assuaged* when she returns.

Audacious: outrageous, daring

How dare he!

Example
Someone who is *audacious* is bold or daring, often in a rude way.

An audacious feat
Evel Knievel was a motorcycle rider who attempted many outrageous jumps. He is remembered for his *audacious* and daring acts.

Bombastic: something that sounds important but really isn't

Example
A person can speak in a *bombastic* way.

Bombastic tales
The history professor knew a lot about history, but he often talked about himself. He said he had many experiences with famous people, including movie stars and presidents. His stories were *bombastic* and tried to make him seem more important than he was.

Capricious: changing quickly for no reason

Example
A person who changes her mind suddenly, for no clear reason, might be described as *capricious*.

On a whim
Jan's friends cautioned her not to be *capricious* when making decisions. She had a bad habit of frequently changing her mind.

Coalesce: to come together

kō-ə-ˈles

Example
Something that *coalesces* comes together as a whole. An orchestra might *coalesce* as a unit after practicing many times.

The team comes together
The soccer team had strong players, but they did not play well together at first. It took about six months before the players *coalesced* as a team.

Congruent: equal or "matched up"

Example

Two angles in geometry can be *congruent*. This means they are equal in size. People can also behave in ways that are *congruent* with their feelings. Their behavior matches up with what they are feeling.

Congruent lines

If two lines are both six inches long, the lines are *congruent*. In other words, they are equal.

Practice 1 – Fill in the Blank

Directions

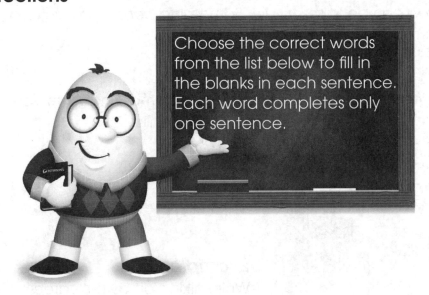

Choose the correct words from the list below to fill in the blanks in each sentence. Each word completes only one sentence.

Words

A. apprise

B. adroit

C. audacious

D. coalesce

E. capricious

F. acquiesce

G. antithetical

H. assuage

Sentences

1. The counselor was able to _____ the patient's fear.
2. The weather has been so _____ over the last week that it has seemed completely unpredictable.
3. When bargaining for a deal, don't _____ too easily.
4. The stunt driver was totally _____; he performed extremely daring moves.
5. The surgeon was very _____ with his hands.
6. It seemed as if the teenager's beliefs were _____ to everything her parents said.
7. A message was sent to _____ the class of the schedule changes.
8. The voices of the choir seemed to _____ into one beautiful voice.

You'll find the answers at the end of the chapter.

Contrive: to make up

Example
Something that is *contrived* can be false or a lie. Something *contrived* can also simply be "made up" or created, without being false.

Making it up
It can be difficult to *contrive* a story. You have to keep remembering what you made up. If you forget a detail, the story might not make sense.

Copious: a lot, plentiful

That's usually me!

Example
While hiking on a 90-degree day you have to drink *copious* amounts of water.

Plenty of leaves
In October, Frederick noticed he had a *copious* amount of leaves in his backyard. "That's a lot of leaves," Frederick thought. "I wonder how long it will take to rake them?"

Deleterious: bad; having a negative effect

de-lə-ˈtir-ē-əs

Example
Something that is *deleterious* is harmful. It causes injury or damage.

Health food only
It's a good idea to eat healthy foods as much as possible. Junk foods have too many chemicals. Eating these often can have *deleterious* effects.

Diatribe: a long and drawn-out critique that is very negative

Example
A customer might give a *diatribe* complaining to a manager about the store's service.

A harsh critique
People do not like to hear complainers. If someone starts a harsh *diatribe*, you might be tempted to escape!

Didactic: related to teaching; focused on teaching, to the point of being dull

Example
A person can give a *didactic* speech. The speech is focused on teaching.

Too much teaching
The counselor was often *didactic* in dealing with students. She turned every talk into a teaching opportunity. Some students wished she would listen more.

Disseminate: to give out widely

Newspapers **disseminate** news, too!

Example
The news channels on television *disseminate* news stories.

Sharing the news
In the United States, news can be distributed freely. The government does not control how the news is shared. In some countries, governments control how news is *disseminated*. Only certain types of news can be shared.

Eclectic: varied, from many different sources

Example

A person might have an *eclectic* collection of art. The art is varied, from many different artists.

An eclectic collector

Sharon had been an art collector for many years. Her art collection was from many different sources in various media. "What an *eclectic* collection," her friends would say.

Enigma: a puzzle;
something that is difficult to figure out or solve

Example

Some riddles are *enigmas*. They are very tough to solve.

A total mystery

Some people are very quiet and not quick to share their thoughts. They may seem like an *enigma*. They are hard to figure out.

Epitome: the most representative example of something

Example

If a lab student is the *epitome* of a dedicated scientist it means she is the perfect example of how a scientist should act.

In tip-top shape

The skier was the *epitome* of a well-trained athlete. She practiced her sport daily.

Esoteric: very intellectual and hard to understand

Esoteric is an *esoteric* word!

Example

Some vocabulary is *esoteric.*

Heavy intellect

The library contains books on many subjects. Some of them are easy to learn about. Others are much more difficult and hard to understand. Ancient Sanskrit, for instance, is an *esoteric* topic!

Practice 2 – Matching Game

Directions

Here is an exercise to practice what you've learned. Match the words to their definitions below.

Definitions

___ **A.** a puzzle

___ **B.** varied, from many different sources

___ **C.** having a negative effect

___ **D.** intellectual and hard to understand

___ **E.** a long and drawn-out critique that is very negative

___ **F.** the most representative example of something

___ **G.** plentiful

___ **H.** related to teaching

Words

1. diatribe

2. didactic

3. enigma

4. copious

5. eclectic

6. esoteric

7. epitome

8. deleterious

You'll find the answers at the end of the chapter.

Evoke: to bring forth

Example

Seeing a picture of someone you like *evokes* a good feeling.

Bringing forth the answer

As Samantha sat staring at her test, her mind drew a blank. She couldn't remember anything about the Civil War she had learned in her history class. Then, she turned the page and saw a photograph of Abraham Lincoln. It *evoked* the memory of the day her teacher taught about the Gettysburg Address. Sam aced the rest of the test.

Exacerbate: to worsen

Example

Loud noise can *exacerbate* a headache.

So can bright light!

Don't make it worse!

If you get a skin rash, be careful not to scratch it! Scratching may *exacerbate* the problem. It can spread the rash and make the itching worse.

Fallible: Capable of being flawed or wrong

Example
Human beings are *fallible*. They often make mistakes.

Right or wrong?
Lester pointed out to his friend Charlie that Charlie had made a mistake. "I hate to admit that I'm *fallible*," Charlie said. "But, you're right—I was wrong."

Incongruent: not equal; doesn't match up

in ˈkäng-grōoənt

Example
Two things that are *incongruent* don't match up with each other.

It doesn't fit
Jeff came home 15 minutes late on Saturday night. His mother asked him where he'd been. "I was at Ray's house," Jeff said.
"That seems *incongruent* with what I heard earlier," his mother replied.
"What do you mean, Mom?" Jeff asked.
"Your sister said you were with her at Sheila's!"

Inevitable: something that is definitely going to occur; bound to happen

Example
A war can be *inevitable*.

Bound to occur
World War I started in 1914. Many people thought it was *inevitable*. World leaders worked to avoid the war, but it still occurred.

Languish: to do poorly or suffer; to fail to thrive

Example
A person who is ill might *languish* without medical treatment.

Simon fails his test
Simon really hates math. It is his worst subject. This morning, he had a test, and he didn't do well.

"Simon," his dad said, "I think we should get you a tutor. Then maybe you won't *languish* in math so much."

Simon looked relieved. He would rather have a tutor than continue to do poorly.

Loquacious: very talkative

lō-ˈkwā-shəs

Example
Someone who is excited about something might be very *loquacious*, talking about it constantly.

Too many words
Jonah was not looking forward to visiting his Aunt Beth. She was extremely *loquacious*. She talked so much that sometimes even she forgot what she was talking about.

Mitigate: to lessen the effect of something; to reduce or prevent an outcome

Example
If you want to *mitigate* the infection from a cut finger, wash it right away.

Ouch!

Changing the outcome
If someone breaks the law, there may be *mitigating* circumstances. These are factors that make the crime less severe. They can lessen the punishment.

Nebulous: difficult to understand, unclear

Example

A concept can be *nebulous*. That means it's hard to grasp. Some philosophies are *nebulous*.

And that's what I call the irony of the ontological priority of praxis.

Tough to grasp

Alex and Phil were studying physics. "I don't understand what this concept means," Alex told Phil. "It's very *nebulous*." Phil explained the concept to Alex and cleared it right up.

Obliterate: to destroy completely

Example

Obliterate can be used to mean "destroy." But it can also be used to show defeat. If one sports team *obliterates* another, this means the first team won big.

Totally gone

Forest fires can *obliterate* entire sections of a forest.

Practice 3 – Fill in the Blank
Directions

Choose the correct words from the list below to fill in the blanks in each sentence below. Each word completes only one sentence.

Words

A. nebulous

B. exacerbate

C. loquacious

D. evoke

E. inevitable

F. mitigate

G. fallible

H. languish

Sentences

1. Even the textbook had the possibility of being _____.
2. The smell of pumpkin pie was able to _____ memories of the holidays.
3. The salesman was very _____, going over every point in detail.
4. It was _____ that the two neighbors would one day meet.
5. The scientific concept was _____ and hard to explain.
6. With the record-breaking high temperatures, the fruit seemed to_____ on the vine.
7. The lawyer wanted to _____ against any further losses for the company.
8. Nobody wanted to _____ the problem, but it got worse anyway.

You'll find the answers at the end of the chapter.

Pedantic: emphasizing small points of learning to an unnecessary degree

Example
A teacher who is *pedantic* focuses on trivial issues. They emphasize minor details.

Trivial concerns
Radha always won when she played trivia games. She knew a lot of minor facts. Her friends loved game night when she was on their trivia team. When she tried to teach them new games, she could be *pedantic*. That was not so fun.

Perturb: to upset

Example
Someone who criticizes you for making a mistake might *perturb* you.

No kidding!

Devon gets upset
Devon studied ballet with a top ballet teacher. The teacher criticized the dancers for the smallest mistakes. This *perturbed* Devon at every class. She would often leave upset.

Placate: to calm down, to satisfy for the purpose of calming down

'plā-ˌkāt

Example
When you *placate* someone, you stop them from being angry or upset.

For Pete's sake!
Ryan had a parrot who talked very loudly. Sometimes he squawked nonstop. Ryan's little sister couldn't stand the noise. "For Pete's sake, Ryan! Please quiet that parrot!" she said. "Can't you do something to *placate* him?"

Pragmatic: practical

Example
Some theories are good ideas, but they are not *pragmatic*, being hard to put into practice.

Not so pragmatic
Sean was always inventing crazy machines. He invented a machine that would automatically warm up ice cream. This, or course, wasn't *pragmatic* since no one wanted to eat hot ice cream. But he tried to sell it on eBay anyway!

Querulous: complaining

ˈkwer-yə-ləs

Example

People who complain a lot are *querulous*. A *querulous* person often complains by whining.

The complainer

You can usually see a *querulous* person coming a mile away. They complain about everything. No matter what happens, it's always wrong.

Sagacious: wise

Example

Some business leaders are *sagacious*. They understand people and know exactly how to solve business problems.

Some fictional characters are **sagacious**, too!

A wise wizard

In the Harry Potter movies, Professor Dumbledore is a *sagacious* wizard. He helps Harry through a lot of messes.

Soporific: something that causes sleep

Example
A boring speech can be *soporific*. It puts you to sleep!

Puts me to sleep
Bedtime stories are often *soporific*. That is the point—they put you to sleep!

Sovereign: a ruler;
to be in charge of oneself, self-directed

Example
The United States is a *sovereign* country. It has an independent government.

Sovereign liberty
It's possible to be free without being *sovereign*. When the settlers came to America, they were free to live where they chose, but they did not govern themselves. The American Revolution was fought to give the colonists *sovereignty* and free them from the English monarchy.

Tacit: understood without communicating

Example

Some good friends have a *tacit* understanding of each other. They know what each other will do, even if they don't talk about it.

It's understood

Chess is a game of strategy. You must trap your opponent's king. Because the king is so important, he must always be protected. It is *tacitly* understood that both players will protect their kings.

Voracious: extremely hungry

Example

If you haven't eaten all day, you might be *voracious* by dinner.

Some teenagers are **voracious** all the time!

I'm starving!

My brother has a *voracious* appetite. He eats enough for two or three people. Be prepared if you take him out to dinner. You might have a huge bill!

Practice 4 – Matching Game

Directions

Here is an exercise to practice what you've learned. Match the words to their definitions below.

Definitions

___ **A.** wise

___ **B.** to upset

___ **C.** practical

___ **D.** something that causes sleep

___ **E.** complaining

___ **F.** understood without communicating

___ **G.** to calm down

___ **H.** extremely hungry

Words

1. querulous

2. tacit

3. placate

4. sagacious

5. voracious

6. perturb

7. soporific

8. pragmatic

You'll find the answers at the end of the chapter.

Answers & Solutions

Practice 1 – Fill in the Blank

Check your answers against the solutions below.

Answer Key

1. H
2. E
3. F
4. C
5. B
6. G
7. A
8. D

Explanations

1. **The correct answer is H.** *Assuage* means to calm. The counselor could *assuage* the patient's fear.

2. **The correct answer is E.** *Capricious* means to change quickly for no reason. The weather has been so *capricious* over the last week that it has seemed completely unpredictable.

3. **The correct answer is F.** To *acquiesce* is to give in. When bargaining for a deal, don't *acquiesce* too easily.

4. **The correct answer is C.** *Audacious* means outrageous or daring. The stunt driver was totally *audacious*; he performed extremely daring moves.

Letting me drive is an **audacious** move for some.

5. **The correct answer is B.** *Adroit* means skilled or nimble. The surgeon was very *adroit* with his hands.

6. **The correct answer is G.** *Antithetical* means opposed to. It seemed as if the teenager's beliefs were *antithetical* to everything her parents said.

7. **The correct answer is A.** To *apprise* means to notify. A message was sent to *apprise* the class of the schedule changes.

Today's class will be held at Starbucks.

8. **The correct answer is D.** To *coalesce* means to come together. The voices of the choir seemed to *coalesce* into one beautiful voice.

Practice 2 – Matching Game
Check your answers against the solutions below.

Answer Key

1. E
2. H
3. A
4. G
5. B
6. D
7. F
8. C

Explanations

1. **The correct answer is E.** *Diatribe* means a long and drawn-out critique that is very negative.
2. **The correct answer is H.** *Didactic* means related to teaching.
3. **The correct answer is A.** *Enigma* means a puzzle.

An **enigma** is something that is difficult to figure out or solve.

4. **The correct answer is G.** *Copious* means a lot or plentiful.
5. **The correct answer is B.** *Eclectic* means varied, from many different sources.
6. **The correct answer is D.** *Esoteric* means highly intellectual and hard to understand.

7. The correct answer is F. *Epitome* means the most representative example of something.

I am the **epitome** of a talking egg.

8. The correct answer is C. *Deleterious* means bad or having a negative effect.

Practice 3 – Fill in the Blank
Check your answers against the solutions below.

Answer Key

1. G
2. D
3. C
4. E
5. A
6. H
7. F
8. B

Explanations

1. **The correct answer is G.** *Fallible* means capable of being flawed or wrong. Even the textbook had the possibility of being *fallible*.

2. **The correct answer is D.** *Evoke* means to bring forth. The smell of pumpkin pie was able to *evoke* memories of the holidays.

3. **The correct answer is C.** *Loquacious* means very talkative. The salesman was very *loquacious*, going over every point in detail.

4. **The correct answer is E.** *Inevitable* means something that is definitely going to occur. It was *inevitable* that the two neighbors would one day meet.

5. **The correct answer is A.** *Nebulous* means difficult to understand or unclear. The scientific concept was *nebulous* and hard to explain.

6. **The correct answer is H.** *Languish* means to do poorly or suffer. With the record-breaking high temperatures, the fruit seemed to *languish* on the vine.

I seem to **languish** in study hall.

7. **The correct answer is F.** *Mitigate* means to lessen the effect of something. The lawyer wanted to *mitigate* against any further losses for the company.

8. **The correct answer is B.** *Exacerbate* means to worsen. Nobody wanted to *exacerbate* the problem, but it got worse anyway.

Practice 4 – Matching Game

Check your answers against the solutions below.

Answer Key

1. E

2. F

3. G

4. A

5. H

6. B

7. D

8. C

Explanations

1. **The correct answer is E.** *Querulous* means complaining.

2. **The correct answer is F.** *Tacit* means understood without communicating.

3. **The correct answer is G.** *Placate* means to calm down or to satisfy for the purpose of calming down.

To **placate** a baby, you might play soothing music.

4. **The correct answer is A.** *Sagacious* means wise.

5. **The correct answer is H.** *Voracious* means extremely hungry.

6. **The correct answer is B.** *Perturb* means to upset.

7. **The correct answer is D.** *Soporific* means something that causes sleep.

8. **The correct answer is C.** *Pragmatic* means practical.

Chapter 5

Prefixes, Suffixes, and Roots

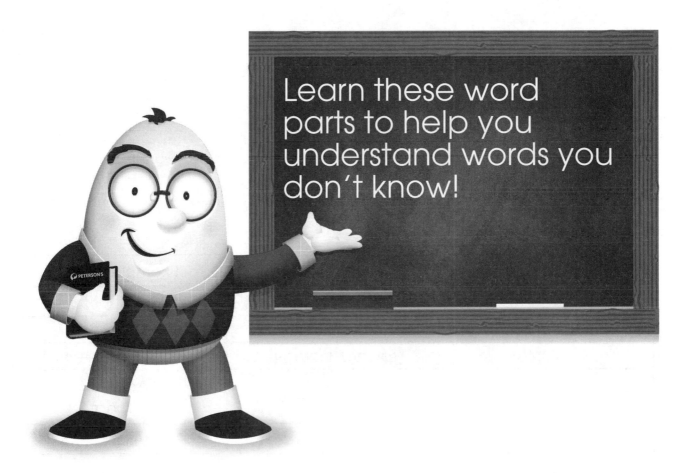

Learn these word parts to help you understand words you don't know!

Prefixes

In addition to learning whole words, it can be helpful to learn parts of words. These can help you guess what new words mean.

Prefixes come at the beginning of words. Here are common *prefixes*.

Prefix	Definition	Example Words
A-	Without	Apathetic
Ab-	Away	Abstain
Ac-	Toward, Increase	Accessible
Ad-	Toward, Increase	Adhere Advocate
Al-	Toward, Increase	Allude
Ap-	Toward, Increase	Apprehend Apprise
As-	Toward, Increase	Assert
Anti-	Opposite of	Antithetical
Co-	Together	Coalesce Cohesive

Prefixes, Suffixes, and Roots

Prefix	Definition	Example Words
Com-	With, Jointly	Compatible Complement Comply Compromise
Con-	With, Together	Conform Context
De-	Away, Down, Undo	Deficient Delete Detach
Di-	Through, Across, Apart	Diverge Diverse
Dis-	Out of, Remove	Dismiss Dispel Dispense
Dis-	Separate, Apart from	Discern Discord Discriminate Disparity Dispute Distinct Distinguish
Em-	Provide, Cause	Embellish
En-	Into, Cause	Enhance
Ex-	Out of	Exclude Exempt
Extra-	Addition to, Beyond	Extraneous Extravagant
Im-	Not	Impede
In-	Not	Incongruent Indecisive Indifferent Inept Inhibit

Prefix	Definition	Example Words
In-	Into	Incorporate Indulge Inherent Innate Integrate Invoke
Ob-	Against, Reverse, Blocking	Obscure Obstinate Obliterate
Op-	Against	Opponent
Per-	Through, Very, Complete	Persistent Pervasive
Pre-	Before	Precede Precedent Presume
Pro-	In favor of, Forward	Propensity Proponent Provoke
Re-	Again	Reconcile Redundant Resilient
Re-	Against	Rebuttal Refute Repress Repulse Restrain Retaliate
Sub-	Beneath, Less, Almost	Subsidize Subtle
Under	Below, Less than	Understatement

Suffixes

Suffixes come at the end of words. Here are common *suffixes*.

Suffix	Definition	Example Words
-able	Can be	Culpable Inevitable Vulnerable
-acy	Quality of	Bureaucracy
-al	In relation to, Action of	Antithetical Beneficial Cerebral Conventional Cynical Frugal Liberal Jovial Marginal Plural Potential Rebuttal Skeptical Substantial Trivial
-ance	Condition of	Enhance

Suffix	Definition	Example Words
-ant	Representative of	Malignant Redundant Relevant
-ate	State of being	Alleviate Animate Articulate Calculate Captivate Collaborate Cultivate Debilitate Differentiate Discriminate Disseminate Dominate Elaborate Exacerbate Exasperate Formulate Imitate Incorporate Innovate Integrate Mitigate Moderate Obliterate Obstinate Placate Procrastinate Proliferate Retaliate Speculate Terminate
-cy	Quality of	Fallacy
-ence	State of being	Consequence

Suffix	Definition	Example Words
-ent	Representative of	Ambivalent Beneficent Benevolent Cogent Coherent Congruent Deficient Diligent Eloquent Expedient Fervent Incongruent Indifferent Inherent Malevolent Opponent Persistent Precedent Prevalent Proponent Prudent Resilient
-er	Action of	Bolster Foster Prosper Waiver Waver
-ible	Can be	Accessible Compatible Gullible Plausible

Suffix	Definition	Example Words
-ic	Quality of, Pertaining to	Aesthetic Altruistic Apathetic Authentic Bombastic Chaotic Charismatic Didactic Dogmatic Domestic Eclectic Erratic Esoteric Fanatic Lethargic Pedantic Pragmatic Soporific Sporadic Toxic
-ify	To become	Exemplify Qualify
-ile	Having properties of	Versatile Volatile
-ious	Having properties of	Atrocious Audacious Capricious Copious Deleterious Loquacious Sagacious Tedious Tenacious Voracious

Prefixes, Suffixes, and Roots

Suffix	Definition	Example Words
-ise	Become	Enterprise
-ish	Having properties of	Lavish
-ist	Representative of	Optimist Pessimist
-ity	State of	Animosity Disparity Identity Propensity
-ive	Possessing quality of	Cohesive Comprehensive Definitive Impulsive Indecisive Pervasive Tentative
-ize	Become	Antagonize Plagiarize Scrutinize Subsidize
-ment	Action of	Complement Compliment
-or	Representative of	Benefactor

Suffix	Definition	Example Words
-ous	Having properties of	Ambiguous Autonomous Boisterous Duplicitous Extraneous Nebulous Pious Querulous Rigorous Spontaneous
-sion	Having quality of	Illusion
-tion	Having quality of	Discretion Intuition
-y	Composed of, Possessing	Arbitrary Contemporary Empathy

Roots

Roots are the main part of words. Here are common word *roots*.

Root	Definition	Example Words
Ambi	Both of	Ambiguous Ambivalent
Anim	Life	Animate
Art	Skill	Articulate
Aut, Auto	Self	Authentic Autonomous
Bene	Well, Good	Benefactor Beneficent Beneficial Benevolent
Col	Together, Jointly	Collaborate Colleague
Corp	Body	Incorporate
Domus	House	Domestic
Domin	Master	Dominate
Du	Two	Duplicitous
Epi	Above	Epitome

Root	Definition	Example Words
Ept	Skill	Adept Inept
Err	Mistake	Error
Fall	False, Deceive	Fallible
Fer	To bring, To carry	Fervent
Iden	The same	Identity
Leg	Law	Legitimate
Liber	Free	Liberal
Loqu	Talk	Loquacious
Luc	Light	Lucid
Mal	Bad	Malevolent Malignant
Medi	Middle	Mediocre
Meta	Beyond	Metaphor
Nov	New	Innovate Novel
Path	Emotion, Feeling	Apathetic Empathy
Ped	Foot	Pedestrian
Phil	Like	Philanthropy
Pop	People	Popular
Sol	Alone	Obsolete
Spec	See	Speculate
Term	Limit, End	Terminate
Tox	Poison	Toxic
Uni	One	Uniform
Vers	Turn	Versatile
Voc	Voice	Advocate

Chapter 6

Practice makes perfect!

This chapter contains extra practice to challenge you. Remember, practice makes perfect!

Practice 1 – Fill in the Blank
Directions

Choose the correct words from the list below to fill in the blanks in each sentence.

Words
A. identify

B. formulate

C. distinguish

D. elaborate

E. hypothesis

F. diverse

G. errors

H. fanatic

I. elated

J. identity

K. extravagant

L. habitat

M. enhance

N. dominated

O. frank

P. exempt

Q. enterprise

R. excluded

S. foster

T. frugal

Practice Makes Perfect

Sentences

1. Molly and Ollie were twins. They were not identical, so it was easy to _____ them. Plus, one was a girl and the other was a boy.

2. The twins had _____ interests. Molly liked to run and play ice hockey. She was very athletic. Ollie liked to carve wood and listen to music. He was really creative. Both of the twins liked movies, and most importantly, they liked to read.

3. When Molly was home, she liked to read the sports and keep up with her favorite teams. She and Ollie lived in St. Louis. She loved the Cardinals because they always _____ their opponents. They usually scored a lot of runs against them.

4. Molly kept _____ lists of sports statistics about her favorite teams. The lists were detailed and complex. She liked to keep track of how the teams were performing. Ollie thought this was pretty strange. "My sister, the sports geek!" he said.

5. One day Molly came home from school and burst in the door with great news. One of her favorite players had been traded to the Cardinals. Molly was so _____! She walked through the house with a huge smile on her face. "Never have I seen someone so happy about a baseball player," Ollie said. He didn't get it.

6. "This trade should really _____ the Cardinals' batting average," Molly explained. "They'll do even better than they have been."

7. "Sports is such a unique _____," Ollie replied. "It's like no other business. Fans get all excited about the teams, and then they trade players. One day, they're just gone!"

8. "Sometimes the teams can make _____ in their trades," Molly admitted. "They can totally get it wrong. But many trades help teams go on to win victories. It's the way baseball does business."

9. Ollie thought about it, but Molly's words didn't change his mind. He thought about his gym class. Sometimes, he wasn't included in a game. When people picked team members, if he got left out, he felt terrible. He didn't like being _____from teams at school. It would be even worse if he were traded to another team!

10. "You've got to understand, Ollie, it's just business," Molly said. "No one is _____ from being traded. It could happen to any player. It's nothing personal."

11. Ollie thought there must be a better way to do business. But he kept his opinions to himself. That's a lesson he learned the hard way. The week before, Ollie was at an _____ birthday party for a friend. There were many platters of food and fancy decorations. Ollie was sure the party was quite expensive. He made a joke that the party probably cost more than picking up a Cardinals' player in a trade. The party hostess glared at him.

12. Ollie immediately felt sorry he'd told the joke about sports. Not only was the hostess upset, but two of his friends used what he said to take jabs at his sister. "You should know, man," one of them said. "Your sister is the sports _____!" A second friend laughed. "She's so into it, it's unreal," he said.

13. Ollie stood there gazing into his drink. He was thinking. He tried to _____ a plan to save both him and his sister from further ridicule. If he joked back, he'd be making fun of his sister. If he didn't, his friends would get the best of him. Finally, he came up with a solution.

14. "Yeah, but she really does well betting on the games!" Ollie said. "Last year, my dad let her make bets for him in the sports pool at his office. Everybody made guesses about who would win the games. My dad and Molly split the winnings. They really cleaned up!"
Ollie's friends looked at him in surprise. Ollie felt proud of his remark. That would teach them to talk badly about his sister.
The next day, Ollie told Molly what had happened at the party. Molly was upset. Ollie didn't get it. He thought she'd be happy that he had stood up for her.
"Do you really want to promote me a gambler, Ollie? Do you really want to _____ that view of me around school? Dad only let me bet on those games in secret. The office didn't even know. It was between him and us!"

15. Ollie was discouraged. He thought he would never understand girls in his whole life. "Molly, can I be _____ with you?" he asked his sister. She nodded yes. She wanted Ollie to be direct and tell her honestly what he thought rather than have him try to deceive her.

16. "I made a joke about the party costing more than traded baseball players. I think I really made the hostess mad. I was nervous, I guess. The party was so fancy it just threw me off my game! I'm so used to being _____ like Mom and Dad. We never spend a lot on parties or going out."

17. "Yeah, Jared told me what you said," Molly replied as she walked in from the kitchen. She had some food for their pet lizard, Cheeky. Cheeky's home looked like an underwater _____ complete with a sunken pirate ship.

18. "Then you know what happened," Ollie said. "I felt pretty awful. Jared made a crack about you being a sports nut. I had to say something to get him back!" "Jared was only kidding," Molly said. "You didn't need to retaliate." The whole thing didn't bother her one bit. She was used to people not understanding her love of sports. "I don't think you were getting him back at all," she said with a knowing sister look. She had another theory why Ollie had said what he said. "I have a _____," she said. "You felt badly because your joke went horribly wrong. You tried to deflect their ridicule away from you by telling them about the bets I did with Dad. Besides, you wished you had won that money. Is it true?"

19. Whenever Ollie tried to hide something, Molly always figured it out. She could _____ whatever he was feeling. She knew him so well. He had been happy for her, but he had wished he'd been in on the bet. Molly was 90 percent of the way toward saving for her new car. He still had miles to go for his.

20. "It is hard sometimes to have this _____ as a sports freak," Molly said. "I know people see me that way. I hear the things they say. But it is just who I am. Sometimes it can be beneficial, like with winning the bets."

You'll find the answers at the end of this chapter.

Practice 2 – Fill in the Blank
Directions

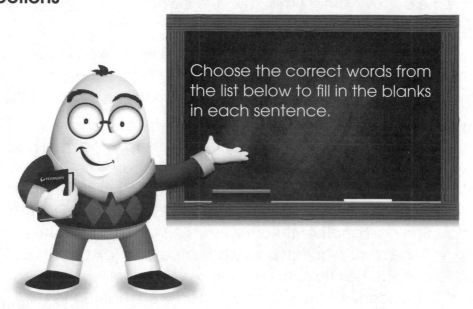

Choose the correct words from the list below to fill in the blanks in each sentence.

Words

A. optimist
B. moderate
C. integrate
D. opponents
E. legitimate
F. mocked
G. intuition
H. incorporate
I. indifferent
J. objective
K. indecisive
L. neglect
M. irate

Sentences

1. Kevin liked working at Montana's feed store because he got to talk about livestock with the customers. He was studying agricultural business in college. He was often asked livestock questions throughout the day as people were shopping. He could _____ what he was learning at school to give better answers.

2. One day, a customer approached Kevin to ask about a piece of equipment for her horse's water tank. It was an item called a de-icer—it kept the water from freezing during the winter. "There are a couple of different types of de-icers," the customer said to Kevin. "Which type works best?" Kevin could tell the customer was _____. She couldn't seem to make up her mind. He gave her as much information as he could. Still, she couldn't choose which one to buy.

3. After answering about thirty questions, Kevin started to get impatient. He thought the lady would never decide. Just then, Sam Ramsey walked down the aisle and heard their conversation. Sam was the barn manager at a nearby 30-acre ranch. "It really doesn't matter which de-icer you use," Sam said to the customer. "They all work the same." Sam was clearly _____ about the products. He didn't feel strongly about any of them. He seemed to know what he was talking about. The lady picked up one of the de-icers, paid for it, and left.

4. Kevin was eager to find out how Sam got to the heart of the matter. He wanted to _____ the rancher's approach the next time he had to answer a customer's questions. "How did you do that, Sam?" Kevin asked. "I answered thirty questions, but that didn't help at all. You just made one point, and she listened!"

5. "It was _____, my boy," Sam said. "I just had a hunch. If I told her they were all the same, she'd probably listen. And she did!"

6. Kevin was surprised that the customer believed Sam. She didn't seem to listen to anything he said. "You looked almost _____ when I walked up," Sam said. "It seemed you were already angry. I've had enough customers to know that just makes it worse."

7. "I had a _____ reason for being angry," Kevin said. "She was a real pain!" Sam smiled and reminded Kevin of what Mrs. Montana always said. "The customer is always right, Kevin." He turned away and brought his purchases to the register. Kevin was grateful for the lesson in customer service. He hoped to have his own store one day.

8. Maria was working hard to prepare a cake for her friend Serita's birthday. Their whole group of friends would be there. The last time Maria had made a cake, it was a flop. The cake sunk down in the pan and looked like a piece of mush. Maria's friends threatened to send pictures of it to CakeWrecks.com. "What's that?" Maria asked. "It's a website where they put photos of all the funny cakes that turned out to be disasters," her friends explained. Maria felt embarrassed. She didn't like to be _____; it took a long time to make that cake, and she didn't appreciate people making fun of her for doing it. She knew her friends were just having a good time, but their laughter still stung.

9. "C'mon, Maria," Serita had said. "Don't take yourself so seriously. So what if you messed up the cake? You can make another one that's better!"
Maria tried again for Serita's birthday. This time, she chose a recipe that was much easier. Instead of making a really difficult cake, she would make something more _____. It might not be as exciting, but at least it would look good!

10. Maria greased the pan with lots of butter and set it aside. As she gathered the other ingredients, she was careful not to _____ the greased pan as it sat waiting for her on the stove.

11. "The _____ is to make a good cake for Serita," Maria reminded herself. "That's the goal. It doesn't have to be super fancy.

12. Maria really enjoyed baking, even though she wasn't that great at it. She liked to learn by watching the baking shows on TV. Sometimes there were contest shows where teams baked together. The baking team _____ would compete for the judges' votes.

13. When Maria watched those shows, she saw she wasn't the only one who took her baking seriously. Some of the team members got very upset when they lost. Maria made mistakes all the time when she baked. But she was an _____. "Look on the bright side," she thought, "I've got a lot of time to get better."

Answers & Solutions

Practice 1 – Fill in the Blank
Check your answers against the solutions below.

Answer Key

1. C
2. F
3. N
4. D
5. I
6. M
7. Q
8. G
9. R
10. P
11. K
12. H
13. B
14. S
15. O
16. T
17. L
18. E
19. A
20. J

Practice 2 – Fill in the Blank

Check your answers against the solutions below.

Answer Key

1. H
2. K
3. I
4. C
5. G
6. M
7. E
8. F
9. B
10. L
11. J
12. D
13. A